Fired!

Tales of the Canned, Canceled,
Downsized, and Dismissed

Written and Edited by Annabelle Gurwitch

A Touchstone Book
Published by Simon & Schuster
New York   London   Toronto   Sydney

TOUCHSTONE
Rockefeller Center
1230 Avenue of the Americas
New York, NY 10020

Copyright © 2006 by Annabelle Gurwitch

TOUCHSTONE and colophon are registered trademarks
of Simon & Schuster, Inc.

For information regarding special discounts for bulk
purchases, please contact Simon & Schuster Special Sales
at 1-800-456-6798 or business@simonandschuster.com.

Designed by Diane Hobbing of SNAP-HAUS Graphics

Manufactured in the United States of America

10   9   8   7   6   5   4   3   2   1

Library of Congress Cataloging-in-Publication Data
Gurwitch, Annabelle.
   Fired! : tales of the canned, canceled, downsized and
dismissed / written and edited by Annabelle Gurwitch.
   p.   cm.
   1. Employees—Dismissal of—Humor.   I. Title.
HF5549.5.D55G87 2006
650.102'07—dc22   2005057591

ISBN-13: 978-0-7432-8985-6
ISBN-10:   0-7432-8985-4

For my guys Jeff and Ezra Kahn,
who haven't fired me yet

Failure is the condiment that gives success its flavor.

Truman Capote

If at first you don't succeed, failure may be your style.

Quentin Crisp

CONTENTS

INTRODUCTION

I didn't want to write this book. If you had told me that one day I was going to be hired and then fired by my idol Woody Allen, I would have jumped from a six-story building to avoid the pain and disappointment. Then if you had told me that because of this experience, I would learn invaluable lessons and grow as a person, I would have jumped from a twelve-story building. Who wants more character-defining experiences! Haven't I grown enough? Apparently not.

In 2003 I was fired from a much-anticipated off-Broadway production. I was completely crushed. I felt humiliated and ashamed. I felt I had two choices: permanently assume the fetal position or go in the other direction and share my experience. I chose the latter and soon greeted everyone from my gynecologist to the lady at the dry cleaners with "Hi, I was just fired by Woody Allen." Well, as it turned out, nothing bored my five-year-old son more than an account of being fired by a cultural icon; however, the response from others was quite different. Friends in the industry assured me that they too had been fired and proceeded to relate their stories. Their humor and insight and generosity consoled me. So I began collecting these tales of jobs gone bad.

I discovered that there are many kinds of stories. There's the job-so-terrible-you-can-only-hope-to-get-fired story. The time-you-got-fired-but-you-didn't-see-it-coming story. The time-you-really-deserved-to-be-fired story, and the time-that-getting-fired-opened-the-door-to-something-much-better-than-you-had-ever-hoped-or-expected-for-yourself story.

If you're reading this book, you've probably been fired, canned, canceled, downsized, dismissed, or—my personal favorite—decruited. It sucks, doesn't it? But after you read some of these tales of jobs gone bad, your story may not seem so terrible. Besides making me laugh, these accounts have truly inspired me. I've known some of the people whose stories appear in this book for years, and yet I had no idea about the crappy "character-building" experiences that contributed to making them into the people I admire. This book also contains a few of the many stories that people from across the country have sent to me.

You may want to write your story down too. I'm not a therapist, but I am an actress and have been in a lot of therapy. Writing your story down can help you bring closure to your experience. In fact, if you want to share your story, visit my Web site, firedbyannabellegurwitch.com.

Someone more clever than I said, "It's not the bounce that counts, it's the bounce back." I agree.

So you were fired. Welcome to the club. We've been waiting for you.

WHO CAME UP WITH THE PHRASE "YOU'RE FIRED"?

It wasn't The Donald. There are a number of legends about how the word *fire* came to mean "to dismiss from employment." Some stories take the fire very literally and attempt to trace the phrase to burning a person at the stake or to burning down someone's house in order to force him or her to leave an area.

Another explanation that seems quite popular on the Internet traces the phrase to a punishment supposedly inflicted on miscreants in the Royal Navy back in the days of sail. The offender, it is said, would be tied over the mouth of a cannon, which would then be fired. While life in the Royal Navy was certainly tough and punishments were severe, including hanging, flogging, and keelhauling (dragging an offender under the ship's keel), there is no truth to this story.

But while the cannon theory may not be literally true, it does touch on what is probably the real source of *to fire*. The verb *to fire* in the "clean out your desk" sense first appeared in the late nineteenth century in the now-obsolete form *to fire out*, as in *to fire out of a gun*. So the phrase *you're fired* almost certainly harks back to the sudden ejection of a bullet from the barrel of a gun to convey the sudden, startling termination of employment.[1]

Webster's Dictionary defines the verb *fire* as 1. to ignite 2. to maintain a fire in 3. to bake in a kiln 4. to arouse, stimulate 5. to detonate or shoot 6. to hurl suddenly and forcefully 7. to discharge from a position.

Synonyms for *fired* include *axed, canned, cashiered, downsized, given the boot, decruited, dismissed, discharged of your duties, made redundant, made at liberty, outplaced, outsourced, pink-slipped, remaindered, replaced, recalled, sacked, terminated, out on your ass, it's just not working out, we're going to have to let you go.*

In Hollywoodspeak, "We've decided to go a different way."
Translation: We found someone more famous than you.

"The director hopes to work with you on something else."
Translation: The director thought you were terrible.

"Artistic differences."
Translation: You're fired.

"We're rethinking the part."
Translation: You're fired.

"It's not you."
Translation: Oh, it's you.

"They love you."
Translation: They never want to see your face again.

"Your script is in turnaround."
Translation: They never want to see your script again.

"The director changed his mind."
Translation: The director is sleeping with a production assistant who will now be playing your part.

Chapter 1

The Job So Terrible You Can Only Hope to Be Fired

Work is the province of cattle.

Dorothy Parker

I do not like work, even when someone else does it.

Mark Twain

I have only been fired once. I was let go from an office job where the boss told me that he was firing me because he wanted someone to work for him who, when he said, "Jump!" would say, "How high?" Ironically, the job was in the offices of the multiple sclerosis society, where the majority of our clients scooted around in motorized wheelchairs.

Rainn Wilson, actor

THAT'S A FACT

Andy Borowitz

I did a number of things in the '80s I'm not proud of. On more than one occasion I shouted out the phrase, "Everybody Wang Chung tonight." But there's one thing I did that was so heinous, I've never told anyone about it. In 1984 I wrote for the TV show *The Facts of Life*.

I'm sure everyone remembers the cultural phenomenon that was *The Facts of Life*. But for those of you who somehow missed it, *The Facts of Life* was a coming-of-age saga about four teenage girls at an exclusive boarding school in Peekskill, New York. There was Blair, the sarcastic beautiful one; Natalie, the sarcastic chubby one; Jo, the sarcastic tomboy; and Tootie, the sarcastic sistah. Watching over all of them was their mentor, Edna Garrett, also known as Mrs. Garrett or, when the girls were in full Fonzie mode, Mrs. G.

Oh, and here's one more piece of *Facts of Life* trivia: It was the worst television show ever produced. Now, given how monumentally it sucked, you may wonder, why did I agree to work on it? Well, quite simply, for the money. You see, I was the sarcastic whore on *The Facts of Life*. But you have to give me a break: I was just out of college, I was broke, I didn't have a car. I had to take the bus, which in L.A. is tantamount to eating out of a Dumpster.

I remember my first day on the show, going in to pitch stories to the producers. These were two middle-aged women charged with the responsibility of making sure *The Facts of Life* did not lose its edge. And the show was at a critical point: It was moving from the safe confines of the boarding school to a whole new setting, a gourmet cheese shop cleverly named Edna's Edibles. It was a move fraught with risk. There was no margin for error. And that was the hornets' nest I was stepping into.

As I sat down in the producers' office, I noticed that they each had coffee mugs with the *Facts of Life* logo on them. I was like, "Cool mugs, where'd you get them?" "Mrs. Garrett gave them to us," one of them explained. It turns out that Charlotte Rae, the actress who played Mrs. Garrett, liked to reward the writers by giving them *Facts of Life* logo mugs, and the better job you did, the more mugs you got. Now, you want to talk about an incentive!

I started pitching my story, entitled "Gamma Gamma or Bust," in which Blair, the sarcastic beautiful one, pulls out all the stops to get into the Gamma Gamma sorority. The producers took it in, chewed it over, and then one of them finally spoke. "It's an interesting story, Andy," she said. "But what's the 'fact'?"

"Say what?" I said.

"The 'fact,' " she said. "Every *Facts of Life* story has a fact, a moral lesson, if you will, a deeper truth that the audience can take away with them."

Suddenly the room started to spin. I realized: They don't know the show sucks. They think they're doing Molière here. And I'm a comedian, I don't really do moral lessons, so I just started spinning my wheels . . . A stitch in time saves nine? Neither a borrower nor a lender be? Finally, with their help, we agreed that the fact of my story would be "Be yourself."

I started to write the script and I thought to myself, I'm going to try something that's never been tried before on *The Facts of Life*: I'm going to write funny things for the girls to say.

I finished it up, handed it in, and didn't hear anything back from the producers for a week. Finally I went up to one of them and said, "Did you get a chance to look at my script?"

"Well, we did, Andy," she said, "and quite frankly, we were disappointed in it."

"What was wrong with it?" I said.

"Well, you didn't get Tootie at all."

I asked her what she meant.

"The way you wrote Tootie, she sounds exactly like Natalie."

I said, "Well, maybe that's because they're both, you know, kind of sarcastic characters."

"They're not sarcastic," she said, genuinely offended. "Natalie is wisecracking and Tootie is sassy. The way you've written them, you can't tell them apart."

And I was like, "Well, the audience will be able to tell them apart because one's fat and one's black." But I didn't say that. Instead I said, "Well, I'll try to fix it in the next draft."

"That's all right, Andy," she said. "We'll take it from here."

All of a sudden I felt something I hadn't felt since I started working there: I cared. I wanted to prove that I could write *The Facts of Life*. I wanted to prove that I "got" Tootie.

Well, as the season wore on, it became clear that the decision to move the show to a cheese shop was an unmitigated disaster. The girls were gaining weight at an alarming pace. To counteract this, the producers removed the muffins and cookies from the snack table and replaced them with carrots, celery, and lettuce. It was like we were being catered by Farmer McGregor. The girls noticed, and they were pissed.

At this point I was given one last chance to prove myself. The producers no longer trusted me to write a script on my own, so they teamed me up with their two pet writers, a team of eager-to-please suck-ups known only as the Two Jims. Our assignment: to write a fantasy sequence set twenty-five years in the future, when Jo, the sarcastic tomboy, would be Jo, a sarcastic high-powered businesswoman.

Now, I thought to myself, finally I'm being given a chance to play to my strengths. No facts, no moral lessons, just unbridled wackiness. So, with the Two Jims' agreement, we wrote a scene in which Jo, inhabiting a futuristic world much like the Jetsons did, attempts a leveraged buyout of Spacely Sprockets.

The producers never told me what they thought of the scene, but the Two Jims later told me that they had been called into the producers' office. "We're very disappointed in the Jo fantasy scene," the producers told them. "But we don't blame you—because we know Andy was in the room when it was written." I couldn't believe it—I had become a cancer on *The Facts of Life*!

Needless to say, I wasn't asked back for a second season, which means I totally missed the arrival of the young George Clooney, who played a sarcastic handyman. But as I cleaned out my office on the last day of work, I noticed a gift box on the desk. I opened it and inside were two *Facts of Life* mugs. Could it be that Mrs. Garrett, in her infinite wisdom, had seen something in me that no one else had? I was so excited, I picked them up and ran into the Two Jims' office—and saw that each of them had received ten mugs.

As I look back on that year, I ask myself, Is there any moral lesson, any deeper truth that we can take away from this? I think it's this: The only thing worse than being a whore is being a whore and totally sucking at it. And that, my friends, is a fact.

After being fired from *The Facts of Life,* Andy Borowitz was "fired up," as often happens in Hollywood, and created the series that launched Will Smith's acting career, *The Fresh Prince of Bel-Air.* He currently writes for *The New Yorker, The New York Times,* and CNN, and is the creator of the very popular Web site and series of books *The Borowitz Report.*

FIRED FACT

Increased risk of heart attack faced by employer firing an employee in the week after wielding the ax: 100 percent.[1]

THE BIG RED SHOE DIARIES

Paul Feig

I was a teenage Ronald McDonald.

The summer after my freshman year of college, I was recruited by Tom Shaker, the director of my local repertory theater, to be a Ronald McDonald. Tom was the Ronald McDonald for the Detroit area and had become famous in the Ronald ranks when the helicopter he was riding in for an appearance hit some power lines as it was landing and crashed upside down in front of a parking lot full of horrified children. Tom crawled out of the wreckage, straightened his red wig, waved hello to the kids, and then proceeded to do his magic show as if nothing had happened. Because of this, he was given the Big Gold Shoe Award by the McDonald's Corporation, an honor that had only been given out once before. I don't know who the previous recipient was, but I have to assume that particular Ronald must have saved his platoon in Vietnam to have topped Tom's accomplishment.

Tom was a big shot in the Ronald world after that, and so when he discovered that nearby Toledo, Ohio, had no Ronald of their own, he easily persuaded his bosses to give him this territory. They agreed, as long as he could find someone to don the red wig whenever he wasn't available. Knowing I was an amateur magician, he immediately recruited me.

He told the McDonald's people that I had been a professional clown for years and would be perfect for the job. The only problem was that I hadn't been a professional clown for years.

I hadn't been a clown ever.

True, I had taught myself to juggle three balls in a simple

pattern, but that was the extent of my experience with professional buffoonery. However, Tom was convinced I could do it and so he put me into full Ronald costume and makeup and drove me down to the corporate offices in Toledo to show them what an amazing Ronald I would make.

As I nervously sat down outside of the boardroom to put on my clown shoes, Tom handed me three colorful balls and told me to walk in, juggle, be funny with the board members, and then get out. He went inside and, just as I finished tying my big red shoes, the boardroom doors flew open and Tom presented me grandly to the room.

I headed in with my mind racing and quickly realized that I had never walked in large clown shoes in my life. I immediately started tripping and catching the fronts of the shoes on the conference room carpeting. I stumbled like a drunk over to the board of directors as my wig slid forward, giving me an Elephant Man–shaped head. Seeing my trouble, Tom quickly started laughing uproariously, as if the inability to walk was part of my clown act. I tripped up to the table and immediately started to juggle. Unfortunately Tom had given me hollow plastic balls that were too light. I might have been able to juggle them with my bare hands, but Ronald McDonald wears gloves, and so the balls went everywhere, one hitting the conference table and bouncing all the way down to the CEO. Once again Tom howled with laughter to indicate that another part of my clown act was incompetent juggling. I then tried to be funny but quickly realized I didn't know what was funny about Ronald McDonald. I'd seen him in commercials for years but had never found him the least bit amusing. He was usually enthusiastic about pushing hamburgers, but I'd never seen him actually make anybody laugh. So, at a loss, I just walked around the table and for some reason turned into a greasepainted Don Rickles. I hurled barbs around the room, making fun of the men's ties and the women's earrings, and I even pinched the fleshy cheeks of the CEO as if he were a fat baby. I then turned and tripped back out of the room, falling out the door and belly flopping onto the carpet. And once again I heard Tom screaming with laughter, conning the board of directors into believing that their new prospective Ronald was a comic genius.

And believe it or not, I actually got the job. I guess finding guys who were willing to be Ronald McDonald was more difficult than I had imagined. And I was about to find out why.

My first appearance as Ronald was at an elementary school on their last day before summer vacation. I was terrified because not only was it my first gig as Ronald but a gang of McDonald's representatives had come down to watch my act. I came out in front of a gym full of rowdy children, for whom the only thing separating them from three months of vacation was me. I quickly started my magic show with a funny trick I had made up the night before. I told the kids I was going to make Chicken McNuggets. I pulled out a pan and slapped on the lid, then said a few magic words. I pulled off the lid and out popped a skinny rubber chicken. The kids all laughed uproariously, and I breathed a sigh of relief.

That was, until I heard a loud voice from the back of the room yell, "Ha ha ha, that's very funny, Ronald, but that's not a Chicken McNugget! Chicken McNuggets are tender and delicious."

I looked up to see one of the McDonald's reps standing at the back of the gym glaring at me as he waved to the kids, trying to cover his anger. I immediately started to sweat, realizing that every trick in my act had been based around some form of making fun of McDonald's food.

As I continued with my show, which I was now desperately

editing on the fly, the kids became restless. The McDonald's reps scribbled notes on their legal pads, as sweat poured from under my wig, turning my clown makeup into a Francis Bacon painting.

By the time I finished, I looked like Alice Cooper, and I knew I had to get out of there.

As I started to head for the door, the principal announced that I, Ronald, was going to give out coupons for free hamburgers, which I had completely forgotten about. In an instant, two hundred kids screamed and rushed me, pushing me into a corner. I desperately tried to hand out the pocketful of coupons as the frenzy grew and the kids ignored the pleas of their teachers to stop crushing me. Fearing for my life, I threw the coupons up into the air. The kids all screamed again and ran to catch the free hamburger vouchers that fluttered down on them like propaganda leaflets dropped over an enemy battlefield. I pushed my way out of the corner, grabbed my magic gear, and ran for the door. Having snatched up all the coupons, the kids turned and saw me fleeing. "Free hamburgers!" they all yelled as they ran after me like the girls chasing the Beatles in *A Hard Day's Night*. I fled through a fire exit, sprinted through the parking lot, and jumped in my Dodge Coronet. Kids were pouring out of the school, screaming and celebrating their release. They saw me and surged toward my car. As I put the Coronet in gear, I saw the head corporate rep for McDonald's push through the kids and bound toward me with a big insane smile on his face.

"Ronald!" he yelled as he ran up, "Ronald, I just wanted to shake your hand!"

He reached in the window and grabbed my hand, squeezing it as hard as he could, like he was trying to break my fingers, then leaned in and hissed angrily in my face, "Ronald—doesn't—drive!"

Believe it or not, they didn't fire me. I wanted them to but they wouldn't. They simply wouldn't fire me because no one else wanted the job and because I was too young to realize I could actually fire myself. My summer turned into a nightmare of parades in which I was mercilessly heckled by the crowd, and in-store appearances at which kids either punched me, pulled off my wig, or burst into tears when I came near. I even got booed when I threw out the opening pitch at a Toledo Mudhens game. Who knew Ronald McDonald commanded so little respect in the real world?

When my Ronald summer ended, I gave Tom back the bright yellow suit, striped socks, big red shoes, and bright red wig and told him I was finished. Like a soldier completing his tour of duty in a war zone, I was retiring back to civilian life in the hopes of putting my battlefield trauma behind me. I had attempted to make children laugh, and I had paid dearly.

You see, sometimes not getting fired is worse than being fired, and to this day, whenever I see a clown, any clown—be he a corporate shill or a birthday clown, dunking-tank fodder or simply one of those clowns you incongruously see driving a dirty old van on the way to some low-paying gig—I always feel sorry for him or her, knowing that the world of kid comedy is a seamy, greasepainted Babylon.

And whenever I see a Ronald McDonald in a TV commercial, surrounded by kids who are paid to pretend that they actually like him and find him funny, I always think, "You poor sucker. They've got you living in a dream world."

Oh, well. At least he's not driving around in a dirty old van.

Yet.

Paul Feig is not driving around in a dirty old van. He created the cult hit TV show *Freaks and Geeks* and is currently directing episodes of the Emmy Award–winning show *Arrested Development* and *The Office*. He is the author of *Kick Me* and *SuperStud*.

FIRED FACT

Two former caretakers for Koko, the gorilla who communicates with humans using sign language, claim they were fired for refusing to "perform bizarre sexual acts" with the famous gorilla, citing Koko's alleged "nipple fetish." They are seeking more than $1 million in damages for sexual discrimination and wrongful termination. Kendra Keller, one of the women suing, was quoted as saying, "Koko's celebrity status doesn't give her a pass for inappropriate behavior."[2]

BIMMY IN TRAINING

Larry Charles

I had just gotten my driver's license but still had never really driven when I got my first job as a cab driver for Yellow Cab in Monticello. Yellow Cab was the biggest cab company in the Catskills and was always in desperate need of drivers. Driver demographics broke down along two lines, lifers (guys who lived in the area, were never leaving, and drank their paychecks away) and guys like me (summer-job types with lives back in the city, girlfriends, college, but who with one false move could easily find themselves doing life behind the wheel of a cab). The cab company was positioned next to the Monticello bus terminal where the "bimmies" landed and would need to be transported to the fading grandeur and dank dilapidation of Catskill resorts still left after the Hasidim and eastern religious cults had, like predators and parasites, taken over the weaker hotels, leaving an entire culture on the brink of collapse. A bimmy was the lowest order of human, an unskilled, usually substance-addicted compulsive gambler who would take the most menial job available at the hotels and last about a week before getting fired. Sadly, years later, I myself was a bimmy, but at this point in my trajectory I still had hope, potential, youth, and ambition.

As I climbed in the driver's seat of that cab on my first day, clutching my clipboard with my fare sheet, Pickles, the particularly sour dispatcher, gave me my first destination. Pickup at Moon Manor, an apartment complex that was home to various strippers, whores, and perverts. I started the engine and pulled out into the street for my first fare and—boom—smashed into an oncoming car. I didn't realize you were supposed to look in that sideview mirror to check for oncoming traffic. *That's* what that mirror was for! I totaled the cab. No words were necessary and none came. The sound of the crash was sufficient. I climbed out the window of the smoking hulk of twisted metal and returned the clipboard to Pickles. I then crossed Broadway to the small rival cabstand across the street, Johnny's Taxi. Johnny, a cool guy, a ladies' man with a dyed black pompadour like Roy Orbison and pointy boots, hired me on the spot. Without missing a beat I climbed into the unoccupied purple cab and headed to Moon Manor.

Larry Charles was working as a valet parker when he got his first job writing on the sketch comedy show *Fridays*. He was a writer and producer on *Seinfeld* and is now directing films and is an executive producer and director on both *Entourage* and *Curb Your Enthusiasm* on HBO.

THE SNUGGERY

Eric Gilliland

The day after I graduated from college, I started a new, exciting grown-up type job. I call it a grown-up job because it was the first job I had that paid me a weekly salary and didn't involve a hat. I had just finished four years at Northwestern University, grappling with *The Cherry Orchard* and *Julius Caesar* and—the quarter I really excelled in—*Star Spangled Girl*. A few weeks earlier Craig, a friend who had been in my acting class, approached me to see if I wanted to work for him. He was making good money, was having a blast, and thought I'd be perfect for this job. The kicker was that it would incorporate many acting exercises we had learned in the last four years, emphasizing group dynamics and such, and, well, I should meet his bosses.

Craig worked for what was, in the mideighties, the most happening, hippest, partyingest nightclub chain in Chicago, where only the sexiest could get past the velvet rope to revel in the most magnificent music and most spectacular light show in the city: the Snuggery. "The Snuggery?" Yes. The Snuggery.

Now, I was never really a nightclub guy. I liked dive bars with old jukeboxes that scratchily played Sinatra and "Dock of the Bay." Evidently, as a twenty-year-old, I lived the exact life of a fifty-nine-year-old divorcé. But Craig wanted to make the Snuggery something different from the average nightclub, and that's why he hired me "against type." His goal was to make the Snuggery an artistically inspired, beautifully realized, loftily essenced fuck den. Craig believed that if the employees all worked together, less as a "team" but more as a "troupe," that wonderful intangible magic associated with theater and the theatergoing experience would disseminate through the club and into the hearts and souls of the incredibly coked-up crowd.

My interview took place in an office that can only be described as early holy-shit-what-have-I-gotten-myself-into. The walls were actually padded, with room-hugging floor-to-ceiling cushions that were covered in designer burlap with bold brown and orange stripes cutting across them. Lots of ski chalet/recording studio wood paneling covered the rest of the huge room. It just reeked of illicit, icky, eighties-type behavior, none of which I'd ever had access to in the ridiculously white cul-de-sac where I grew up selling lemonade, playing lawn darts, and suppressing my true self in. This room was uncomfortably cool and evil. And in the corner—I'm not kidding—a hot tub. Craig thought this was the ultimate sign of having "made it." I thought this was an office you'd associate with the bad guys on *Baretta* . . . whose interior designer was heavily influenced by Rhoda's apartment.

I don't remember much of the interview besides meeting one of the managers and thinking he was creepily slimy and really, really thin. Like runner thin. Of course now that I look back on it, I don't think he was much of a runner. Looking back, I think his veins would have collapsed if he had dialed a number that included the extra three digits of a different area code. But back then I thought, Hm. Svelte.

I somehow won them over with a quality that I still have. Back then it was called "boyish charm." Now it's called "cloying" and "sad." I was told that next week, after I became a college graduate, I was to start my training in my new position as dynamics manager for the Morton Grove Snuggery. Which is just a horrible collection of proper nouns.

A dynamics manager was basically in charge of "fun." My job, every night, was to throw the most exciting party in town.

But in order to throw this astounding party, I had to wrangle many elements. First and foremost I had to take a ragtag group of waitresses and bartenders and doormen and unite them as a team—no, a troupe—and make sure that through their excitement and commitment, everyone who came through those doors would be certain to have, unequivocally, the Best Night of Their Lives. We were the folks who would make people's dreams come true, fulfill their wishes, make this night so special that they would find it worthy of drinking until they puked in a urinal and then get back to the bar in time for the sixth round of Goldschlagers. Because that would then be the Best Night of Their Lives. And how does this disparate group of strangers bond together as a united force, committed to providing the Best Night of Their Lives to the wonderful people of this northwest suburb of Chicago? Well, naturally, theater games.

The following Saturday, Craig assembled all the new employees, including me, to fulfill the requirement that anyone who worked at the Snuggery had to go through. Something he called Snug training. (Oh, you'll see the word *snug* used a lot in the next two paragraphs.) For two unpaid hours Craig made everyone, bouncers and bar backs alike, pretend he was, say, an animal. Yes, that's right, Tony, you're a bear! A big grizzly bear! What do you sound like? How do you walk? What do you think of Cynthia over there, who's a . . . what were you again, Cynthia? Right, a woodchuck. What do you think of Cynthia the Woodchuck, Tony the Bear? Well, it was all horribly embarrassing to see what people will go through just to get a job. Now that I've been in television for fifteen years, this of course is routine for me to witness. But back then it was shocking.

See, the Tonys and Cynthias of Morton Grove had never been anything more than Tonys or Cynthias. They weren't comfortable being animals or closing their eyes and picturing themselves walking on a beach or throwing imaginary balls to each other that would, according to Craig's shouted orders, suddenly be "Heavy!" or "Light!" They just wanted to serve drinks, beat up a drunk line-crasher or two, have some employee-discounted potato skins, and go home via the White Hen Pantry to grab a twelve-pack of Hamm's or maybe Blatz, drink it in the church parking lot, if it was snowing, do a few doughnuts and maybe skitch a little, zigzag back to their parents' house, stumble in the front door, tip over the aquarium, shout "fuck," get in a fight with their mom about how much they drink, pass out in the family room watching some movie with Dom DeLuise, probably the one where he's trying to kill himself but Burt Reynolds won't let him—wait, Burt wants to kill himself and Dom DeLuise won't let him—wake up to the sound of their father consoling their mother as she cries because she didn't know her kid says "fuck," say sorry, heat up a waffle, and then go out with Mitch to fix his truck. They didn't want to pretend they were all different mechanical parts of a clock.

I made up my mind then and there that when I became a full-fledged dynamics manager, I wasn't going to humiliate my troupe.

Which was going to be hard.

Throughout the night the deejay was instructed to play certain songs that were cues for all the employees to do somewhat choreographed, "fun" moves that would really get the crowd going. For instance, that was the summer of both the Pointer Sisters' and Van Halen's songs "Jump." Whenever either of them sang "jump" in the song, each and every employee in the place had to stop whatever he was doing and jump in place. "Jump!" Jump. "Jump!" Jump. Horrible. Or, say, when the song "Freeze-frame" came on, whenever the words "freeze-frame" were sung, everyone had to freeze in place. "Freeze-frame!" Hold it . . . move. "Freeze-frame!" Hold it . . . move. It was particularly sad to watch Tovar, the Armenian busboy, participate in all of this. These special songs were called Snug tunes. And I had to make sure everyone who worked there performed them. I was doomed.

And to add to the horror, I did all this wearing the official Snug outfit: tuxedo shirt, unbuttoned at the top but still with a wraparound bow tie, and slick, water-repellant, multi-zipper-pocketed parachute pants.

At first things went along fine. I did my job. I could get any-one I wanted in the club, drinks were free, food was free, and I'd get free tickets to the big summer SnugFest with live bands and big-name comedians. I was at the white-hot center of all things hip and exciting in the world of Chicago nightlife. The prob-lem was I don't like most things hip and exciting. That's a big something to realize when you're twenty-one. And then, evi-dently, relearn every three years or so for the rest of your life.

I never should have been there in the first place.

And when your heart checks out, so does your brain, and I started to really, really suck at my job. The last straw, as I recall, was when I misscheduled either the Pajama Party Night or the Love Connection Theme Night. Whichever it was, it didn't sit well with Scarface and his drugged-out minions up in the hot tub.

I knew word had gotten back that I was slacking off because when I got to work that night, I could feel something had shifted. Something was in the air. That heavy sense of impend-ing unemployment. And once you get that stink on you, all your former buddies who thanked you for "being cool" with all those forced antics quickly turn away and shun you, making you, suddenly, persona Snug grata.

Craig took me aside, out into the alley behind the kitchen. He looked at me, eyebrows akimbo, and said, "Ah . . . Eric . . ."

"I'm fired, aren't I?" I beat him to the punch. No one should have to go through the agony of firing a friend. We both knew it was going to happen. And I was absolutely fine with that.

Sorta. True, I was released from an astoundingly soul-sucking job, but then again, the upshot is I failed. People paid me to do something, I didn't do it well, and I got fired. And getting fired doesn't feel good. What was more humiliating: being forced to wear my Snug outfit, or being forced to not wear my Snug outfit? I wasn't going to miss the place, and yet I didn't feel great leaving. The rest of that summer I prepared to leave home for Hollywood and spent my nights in dingy dive bars, listening to Sinatra and "Dock of the Bay."

Eric Gilliland is a writer and producer and holds the distinction of being the only executive producer who wasn't fired during his tenure on *Roseanne*.

FIRED FACT

In 1876 Vincent van Gogh was fired from his job in an art gallery in Paris. He was fired again in 1879 while under contract as an evangelist. Van Gogh fired his ear in 1888.[3]

BRUCE CAMERON
REMODELS YOUR REDUNDANCY

I wanted to be my generation's John Steinbeck. Instead it seems that I turned out to be my generation's Erma Bombeck. Without the dress.

Until my first book was published in 2001, I made virtually nothing as a writer, so I was forced to seek employment because my parents had the audacity not to be Rockefellers. I ran a software company. I was a repo man. One of my first jobs was driving an ambulance in Kansas City. The job required me to watch hours and hours of television and then drive around town at breakneck speeds, which I was perfectly suited for because that's exactly how I had spent my senior year of high school. During that same period in my life, I cleaned apartments for a guy who owned what I suppose could charitably be called a slum. Tenants would move out, and I would go in and scrub sinks, paint walls, and remove dead bodies. That's the first job I ever got fired from. I ran a dishwasher using laundry detergent and created enough foam to make a runway safe for a flaming airliner. Believe it or not, I didn't actually know I was fired when my boss said I wasn't cut out for the job. I thought that had been obvious all along. Eventually, though, I noticed he had quit calling me.

I was also fired from a job at a radio station. I was hired to supply comic relief on a call-in show in the coveted Saturday noon hour. The show sucked. Even my kids were too embarrassed to call. They were afraid someone might hear them and they'd have to transfer to a new school district. I said, "Who's going to hear you? No one's listening!" When I was finally let go, the reason I was given was "It's a comedy show with no comedy and a call-in show with no calls." I guess I wasn't cut out for the job.

Not long after that I became the human resources director of a large software company. I was hired to create a new employee benefits package but then the company's stock imploded and we had to cut 60 percent of the staff, so the only employee benefit they got was that they were fired. I personally fired over three hundred people, and I got pretty good at it. My friends have said I have a "dark gift," because instead of getting angry, most of the people I fired seemed worried for *me*. A lot of the terminated employees would say, "Bruce, are *you* going to be okay?"

When I would fire someone, I would always use the phrase "as you know" to start every sentence. "As you know, the company is downsizing . . . As you know, profits are down . . . As you know, we're making some cutbacks." They'd be nodding, and when I said, "So we're going to have to let you go," they'd say, "I know."

What I learned from all this is that when the HR director says, "As you know . . ." stand up and run out the door. They can't fire you if they can't catch you. One employee used this technique to evade termination for more than a year. When he heard we wanted to talk to him, he went home sick. Then he went on vacation. Then he went on disability—for sleep apnea! Basically he couldn't come to work because he was snoring. When he was in the office, he was always with a client. We just couldn't fire the guy. Then the boss's daughter got married and the guy went to the reception, figuring that no one would fire someone at his own daughter's wedding. He was wrong.

I eventually got fired from the HR job at the software company, which was no surprise. The person who did it didn't have the dark gift, though. I wound up being sort of angry. Instead of using the "as you know" method, he pretty much implied that the reason our company was losing so much money was me.

He also told me I wasn't cut out for the job. Ironically, that was truly the only job I didn't deserve to get fired from.

Bruce Cameron is now enjoying his career as a syndicated columnist and the best-selling author of *8 Simples Rules for Dating My Teenage Daughter* and *How to Remodel a Man*.

FIRED FACT

Percentage of workweek the typical worker spends in meetings: 25.

Odds that a person at a meeting doesn't know why he's there: 1 in 3.[4]

DON'T CALL ME, I'LL CALL YOU

Judy Gold

One of the first jobs I wasn't asked back to was as a toll collector on the New Jersey Turnpike. That was a bit humiliating because being a toll collector cannot by any stretch of the imagination be called a demanding job. Basically, you're a supermarket cashier who rings up one item all day long. I was eighteen when I worked as a toll collector during the summer after my freshman year at college. There were three shifts: 6:30 A.M.–2:30 P.M., 2:30 P.M.–10:30 P.M., and then 10:30 P.M. until 6:30 A.M. My shifts would change every week depending on who was taking a vacation. I was the only woman working most of the time, and I was very young, thin, with a Barbra Streisand '80s perm that I didn't need because I have naturally curly hair, and I looked pretty hot in my New Jersey Turnpike uniform. There were many times when my lane would have a long line of trucks and everyone else's lanes would be empty because the truckers would get on their CB radios and alert the drivers that there was a chick in lane six. That way they could pay the toll and then I could direct them to the nearest truck stop so they could jerk off. I thought if truckers were that desperate to see a pair of boobs in that outfit, then their jobs were even crappier than I originally thought.

The best perk of that job was that every day someone would mistake a ten or a twenty for a dollar bill, and by the time I would be finished making change, they'd already have driven away. I'd put the money aside until the end of the day. If nobody claimed it, I'd keep it. I called it my marijuana money. One time a person gave me a twenty and drove away. I leaned out of the booth, but he had already gone. I put the money aside and then about a half hour later, he came back asking for his change. I got reprimanded for not trying hard enough to alert him to his mistake. Apparently I was supposed to report it to the supervisor as soon as it happened. I guess they wanted me to run down the highway waving nineteen dollars over my head yelling, "Come back!" while getting hit by a car. Needless to say, I had a different job the next summer.

The summer before my senior year in college, I got a job as a waitress in a Mexican restaurant. I just loved the job. I got huge tips because I would make the tables laugh, I would tell them which items sucked on the menu, and I was very attentive to the customers. This was my first real "performing" job. I was also happy to party after work and sleep as late as possible. Thus I overslept and ended up missing a staff meeting at the restaurant. What we did at the staff meetings, I can't recall. We probably talked about which door to push when entering and exiting the kitchen, how to wrap the silverware in napkins, or what refried beans actually were. They had hired a new manager who was a tall, androgynous woman. Let's just call her Janet Reno. I could tell she didn't like me. Even though she was nice to me, I got a feeling when I was around her that something was up. I got lots of attention from the customers and staff, plus I was taller and younger than her. Tall women have this huge unspoken competition. The night after the missed staff meeting, I got to work, and Janet Reno told me that I was fired. I was so upset. I was fired! There were no ifs, ands, or buts. It wasn't any passive-aggressive thing where they just stopped putting me on the schedule, I was flat-out fired. I felt like total shit—like a huge loser—and I went out and bought a calendar for the first time so I could write down my appointments. Now whenever I get my Janet Reno feeling, I trust it, and, as it turns out, it comes in handy.

One of my first good-paying jobs as a performer was doing warm-up. I loved it. It kept me on my toes and it kept me off the road. I got a job doing the warm-up for a new show called *Women Allowed*, on what was then called the Comedy Channel. Mo Gaffney was the host and she was amazing. It was a talk show that featured mostly women and dealt with women's issues. The show had great guests. I remember one show with Queen Latifah and her mom.

I would go out there and tell my stupid jokes before they started taping, during the breaks, and whenever there was some sort of technical difficulty. My big number was that I would get the audience to sing the *Brady Bunch* theme, and I would look around like I was in the boxes. I talked to the audience, I told jokes about my mom, and I would always get a great response. I remember one of the executives bringing me into her office—she's a huge *macher* now—and saying to me, "You know, Judy, the happiest part of my day is when you arrive here. I just know I'm gonna laugh." I was in high heaven. After all, this was steady work and I was making enough to get health insurance. A few times, during some breaks, audiences yelled, "We want Judy!" I was feeling really confident. I just loved this job!

The show went on hiatus for a few months, so I booked myself on the road for that time. When the hiatus was over and the shooting was about to start, I waited to hear when they would be needing me. The longer I waited for the phone to ring, the more I recognized that familiar feeling I had had with Janet Reno at Marita's Cantina in New Brunswick, New Jersey.

I had waited long enough. I decided I was going to make the call. I called the producer. I don't think she took my call the first time, which I know is shocking, but eventually she got on the phone. I had rehearsed what I was going to say. "Hey, I was wondering when you'd be needing me for warm-up so that I could book myself accordingly."

She replied, "I think we're going to try someone new this time around."

"Oh, okay," I said.

"It's just that you do the same material every show, and we want some new material."

New material? What the fuck is that supposed to mean? I wanted to say, "What, am I supposed to write an entirely new act for each taping? Each show has a different audience, asshole! Are you mental? Every comic does the same shit every show."

So I said, "Oh. Great. Okay. Thanks." I was devastated. My first showbiz firing, but of course it wasn't really a firing, it was the cowardly Hollywood kind of firing. God forbid they would actually call me to tell me they weren't bringing me back. It's nice the way television executives, who usually have nine hundred cell phone numbers, and personal assistants eager to look up a number and dial it for them, suddenly become incapable of making a phone call when they have to notify a person that their services are no longer needed. No, this way I got the chance to call and look like a huge asshole begging for work.

I've run into Ms. Executive several times since then. She'd be executive-producing a show and my manager or agent would call and she would be like, "Oh, I love Judy, she's the best!" She was my first real glimpse at the cowardly, passive-aggressive way executives treat talent.

Now, sometimes you actually deserve to be fired. One of my first jobs out of college was working for a company called Military Media. It was a really riveting job, selling advertising space for military-based newspapers, and I was under the delusion that I was working in publishing and one step away from editing *The New Yorker.* I got there at 9 A.M. and by 11:30 I was finished with all of my work for the day. Having way too much free time on my hands, I would call a sex line, transfer the call to other people's phones, and then run over to their cubicles to see their reaction. Of course everyone thought I was funny, until I hit the wrong extension and, a few minutes later, was called into the boss's office. I was summarily canned. But I left that job with some compensation. One of my phone sex victims was a girl named Sharon. Sharon Callahan. Sharon and I spent nineteen and one-half years together and have two children, Henry and Ben Callahan-Gold.

Judy Gold hosts *At the Multiplex* on HBO. She appears regularly on Comedy Central and has had comedy specials on HBO, Comedy Central, and LOGO. Her CD is called *Judith's Roommate Had a Baby.*

POOR JUDGMENT

Illeana Douglas

I was once fired as a coat check girl after four hours.

You might ask yourself, as I have many times, How is it possible to be fired hanging coats? I have arms. I know what coats are. I don't come home and throw my coat on the floor. I hang it in a closet. I have experience.

Poor judgment.

I exercised poor judgment in giving a lady her fur coat back when her boyfriend—who I later found out was in the Mafia—asked me not to.

"Don't give her the coat!"

"Give me my coat!"

"Don't you give her that coat!"

"Sir, she seems to want her coat."

"You are dead! You hear me, dead!"

Okay, I didn't die, but I was fired. By my very irate manager, a man who it was said was "mob-connected." I know this to be true because years later he turned up as a "technical adviser" on a movie I was in called *Goodfellas*.

Poor judgment.

I tell this story because it draws a strange parallel to my next story, in which I explain how years later I again exercised poor judgment and got myself fired not once, not twice, but three times in the same day.

I had made a television deal for a script I had developed. When the show was passed on, I was talked into doing another pilot. It was kind of a half-baked idea and I didn't really want to do it, but everyone kept telling me it was going to be great. They'd hired a great director, gotten other great actors; the head of the network even called me to say, "You're going to be great, kid. It's a great life. You'll see." Then he offered me a great deal of money, so I said yes.

Poor judgment.

Sitting by the pool of my newly rented house, I read the script. I tried to imagine how great it was all going to be.

In a panic, I called the head of the network. "Listen," I said. "I have some real concerns about this show. Could we talk about it? Face-to-face."

"Sure," he said, "come down to my office. We'll discuss it."

Poor judgment.

I entered the network head's office. I sat on one couch. He sat on another. He patiently listened to me. "It's like the very thing that's wrong with the show is my character, and just because I'm funny, it doesn't mean that I can make it work, because if it's not on the page, I can't make it funny."

"Are you single?" he said.

"Yeah," I said, and then I continued to give my notes.

Poor judgment.

"The last thing I want is to be standing on that stage in front of all of these great people and this great comic genius director, with egg on my face, because we all realize that this character does not work." That's when he pounced on me and put his tongue down my throat.

Some people take criticism badly. Others just pounce on you and put their tongue down your throat.

At first it was funny. It was like one of those '60s movies where someone chases you around a desk and a couch. Then it was more like a French film with him on top of me on the couch, and finally it was like a '70s disaster movie where I screamed a lot and nobody heard me.

When he finally let me up for air, he said, "So what do you

think?" and I said, "For the head of a network you're some good kisser."

I certainly wasn't going to open my mouth again to give him any more notes. I made a beeline for the door.

"We're going to keep this between you and me, right?"

"Right," I said. "I won't tell anyone you're a good kisser."

He opened the door and let me out.

As I stood in the hall outside his office, it was hard to assess how the meeting had gone. Really well? Maybe. Really badly? Maybe.

His assistant caught up to me at the elevator. "Do you need validation?" she said.

"Yes," I said. "Yes, I do."

She smiled at me. "Your parking ticket. May I have it?"

"Oh," I said. "Sure. Yeah."

She carefully placed six orange validation stickers on my ticket.

The next day I started work.

Remember my conversation pre the pouncing? The show wasn't very good, and I was the opposite of funny. I was in my own afterschool special. "Portrait of the Unfunny."

There I was wiping egg off my face when the director—the comic genius—gave me a sympathetic little smile. Sympathy mixed with pity. Symitty.

He has a very kind face, I thought. Maybe I could tell him I was recently molested and didn't think I could do the run-through. I played the scene out in my head. I imagined him years later at the Friars Club telling his buddies, "Here's one. One time this actress told me she couldn't land her jokes because some poor guy was trying to get a little nookie!" I said nothing.

Poor judgment.

Wednesday's run-through did not go well. That's showbiz talk for "I sucked." The highlight was seeing my boss—the head of the network—and realizing I was going to be his bitch for the life of the series. I asked my costar what she thought of him, but she said, "I've never really spoken to him." Smart girl. Good judgment.

I was fired after the run-through. He personally fired me after he told me that I made him sick, I wasn't funny, and that I wasn't even trying. At first I was confused. I mean, was he talking about the meeting in his office? But then he said, "And if you think I'm going to pay you, you're crazy." This seemed bad. New to L.A. Fired from my first pilot. They weren't going to pay me.

Wait a minute, I thought. I have a manager. We'd handle this together. I called her. What was it she said? Oh yes. "You're fucking fired, you fucking piece of shit. How could you fuck this up, you fucking idiot!" It was about forty-seven *fucks* in a row. "Fucking burning bridges; you'll never fucking work again," and "I'm going to call your agent and I hope he fucking fires you too."

When I got home I called my agent and he got on the phone immediately, which in show business is a really bad sign.

"So what's up?" he said. "What happened?"

It was like the coats all over again. I tried to sound confident. "It was all for the best," I said.

Silence.

"Of course they're going to pay me," I said.

Crickets.

"I haven't burned any bridges," I said.

Tumbleweeds.

I may have even said, "That's the problem in this town— everyone works on fear."

I was terrified. I knew he was going to fire me.

"Listen, Illeana, I can't work with someone . . ." It was just a blur after that, although I never heard the word *fired*. He just kept wishing me the best of luck. It was my third firing of the day, so I kinda got the drift as to where he was going.

I called my lawyer. I called my lawyer because I knew he couldn't fire me. He wasn't even my lawyer. He was actually my ex-boyfriend's lawyer. So in what would seem an extraordinary act of poor judgment on his part, he took my call.

Now, what is crazier than being fired three times in the same day is the fact that I told him this exact same story minus the coat check part. By the end of the week I was paid in full, and because everyone had fired me, I didn't have to pay anyone any commission. The head of the network even called to offer me a miniseries.

"So you'll do the mini, right? Tits and guns, baby! Tits and guns!"

On Friday my entire team called to congratulate, grovel, and rehire me, which in an act of good karma I allowed them to do.

Poor judgment.

Illeana Douglas's memorable work on screen includes her roles in the films *Ghost World*, *To Die For*, and *A Stir of Echoes*. She received an Emmy Award nomination for her turn as Angela on *Six Feet Under*.

Subject: Number One Pooper-Scooper
From: Robert Reich
Date: September 26, 2005, 7:43 A.M., EST
To: firedbyannabellegurwitch.com

Annabelle, I'd love to be fired by Woody Allen. Do you know how many people can say they've been fired by Woody Allen? As to whether you should have told your gynecologist, I don't know your gynecologist and I will probably never meet him, but I think he probably went home and talked about it. There's a certain cachet to the story.

I've had many jobs and I have also been fired.

I had my first job when I was eight. I bought candy wholesale and sold it retail to my friends and I pocketed the difference. Money wasn't the goal—it was candy—and I did very well but I had to fire myself because I blew up like a blimp. I then had a series of summer jobs. At one point I was a gofer at an advertising agency. We were on the twentieth floor of an office building in Manhattan and my boss had a poodle who defecated on the tar roof. It was my job to scrape the poop off the tar in 300-degree heat. I wanted to do a good job and I think I did. After that I went on to other pooper-scooper opportunities. I can say for sure that there is a direct linear connection to my later career. As the secretary of labor, I was the embodiment of a pooper-scooper.

Now, when you're dealing with people with advanced university degrees, people don't usually say, "You're fired." They say, "You don't seem to be happy here; can we talk?" I was working for the solicitor general's office. This was in a Republican administration and I didn't do well. The administration wanted to get rid of the First, Fourth, Fifth, Eighth, and Ninth Amendments to the Constitution. I couldn't really bring myself to get excited about this enterprise. No one said, "You're fired." What they said was maybe I should look for another job, but you know what they mean and they know that you know what they mean and you know that they know that you know exactly what they mean and you leave and say to yourself, "I'm fired and I'd better look for something else."

Of course, sometimes being fired can be wonderful. Being fired can mean you are creative to the point of driving someone crazy. I always tell my students, if you are taking enormous risks and doing things that no one else has thought of, you will eventually be fired. But being fired means different things in different economic classes.

Annabelle, you have a miserable profession: you never know where your next job is coming from, you have to worry about your connections, you're only as good as your last job, it's a winner-take-all business, and every other business is following along in your trail in industries furthest removed from show business. There are no stable jobs and secure incomes anymore. In this economy you can be doing exactly the job you were hired to do and be fired through no fault of your own because companies want to get payrolls down. Now, for some people, this can be dynamic—they enjoy the challenge—but for others, it might be difficult. The next job you get might not pay as much as the job you lost or you might lose your health care and pension when you change jobs. This can be a difficult transition. But this isn't an inevitable situation. There are things we can do if we care about who shares in the circle of prosperity. I mean, we aren't living in the jungle.[5]

P.S. My son is an actor; he's really very funny! Check out his Web site: www.dutchtv.com.

Robert Reich, who was secretary of labor under Bill Clinton and is now professor of public policy at Berkeley, has written lots of books and pontificates endlessly on TV and radio about work and the economy. He's been fired twice and was glad both times because he needed a good kick in the ass.

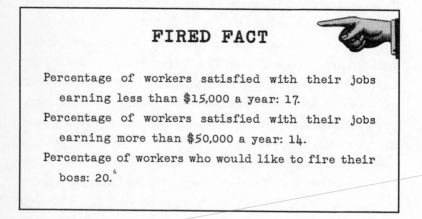

FIRED FACT

Percentage of workers satisfied with their jobs earning less than $15,000 a year: 17.

Percentage of workers satisfied with their jobs earning more than $50,000 a year: 14.

Percentage of workers who would like to fire their boss: 20.[6]

Subject: Nesting
From: Jessica van der Valk
Date: March 12, 2005, 6:32 P.M., PST
To: firedbyannabellegurwitch.com

Broke and fresh out of grad school, I decided to look for a job in the film industry. That hot, exhausting summer, I ran from interview to interview, but four months went by without an offer.

I was desperate. I took in a roommate because I couldn't pay my rent. She was British: an illegal alien with a tourist visa, motorcycle, borderline personality, and one of those lispy home-counties accents that during the initial thirty seconds of exposure sound charming but get annoying really quickly. She wanted a job in the film industry. Since she had no work permit and no skills, I thought she'd be winging her way back to Sussex by the end of the month. But within a week, she had a plum job *in the film industry*.

The next day, I went out to four interviews armed with my resume, a new pair of nylons, and a British accent. I got all four jobs. Stunned, I took the best offer, a job in the literary department of a famous talent agency. Every morning I motored to work muttering "skuht, fuhn, buhd" (the British versions of *skirt, fern, bird*) under my breath. My con was undetectable; even British people thought I was one of them. I had to make up schools I went to and places I had lived in London.

After almost three months of making myself indispensable in my new job, I began to think about "phasing out" my British accent. I was beginning to depend on it too much. All those months of joblessness had taken their toll on my self-esteem. My accent was not just my ticket out of jobless hell, it was my crutch; I was using it in supermarkets when intimidated by the checkout counter personnel and in restaurants with snotty waiter/actors. Since I was a long-term Angeleno, it was possible that I might even run into a high school buddy at work, and then what would I do?

I began, tentatively, experimentally, to phase in emphatically Americanized vowel sounds and let it be known that I was trying to "get rid of my accent." Soon after, my boss, whose twin obsessions were herbal management of her PMS and landing a man, put down the phone long enough to hiss, "What is happening to your accent? You sound almost . . . *American!*"

"Yes," I chirped cheerfully in that day's slightly Anglo-nuanced imitation of Sandra Dee in *Gidget*, "I'm so glad you noticed."

She gave me a squinty glare and within a week told me that she would "have to let me go." When I asked why, she said that I wasn't nesting. My British accent fully revived by panic, I explained that I wasn't a bird. "Well," she said, sounding determined, "you're just not acting like you're staying. You haven't personalized your cubicle with photos or knickknacks."

"You're firing me because I haven't any *knickknacks* in my cubicle?" I thundered.

She nodded emphatically, and so I was fired.

Jessica van der Valk is a dog owner who lives in Van Nuys, California.

When I was sixteen I had a job as a dishwasher at a mom-and-pop place in a strip mall. The mother didn't like me very much because the dad would let me leave early. One day, after arriving at work, I was in the process of locking up my bike in front of the place. I had a really long chain I had to wind around the lamppost, and just as I finished, their ten-year-old son came out and said, "My mom says you don't have to work here anymore." I could see her scowling at me through the window, so I unwound my long chain and rode home. What was there to say to that?

Of course I've been fired as an actor. Once I was fired from a TV show because the producer told me I was "acting too gay," and once I had one line in a pilot and they decided to dub in someone else's voice for my one line! All things being equal, I think I prefer to be fired by a ten-year-old.

Ian Gomez was one of the stars of the TV series *Felicity*. He appeared in the movie *My Big Fat Greek Wedding,* which was based on his real-life wedding to Nia Vardalos.

Chapter 2

The Firing You Didn't See Coming

Comedy is tragedy plus time.

Carol Burnett

If A is success in life, then A equals x plus y plus z. Work is x; y is play; and z is keeping your mouth shut.

Albert Einstein

I was fired from *Saturday Night Live* by fax. No, I'm just kidding. They faxed my agent.

Sarah Silverman

THE LITTLE FUCK THAT COULD

Sandra Tsing Loh

I sat at my laptop the other day, in Zenlike silence. The doorbell was still, fax silent, phone didn't ring. There was nothing to rudely break my concentration, to get between me and my writing, and it was a nightmare. To hell with this! I thought. Oh to return to that one golden month when there wasn't time to be alone with my tedious thoughts, when the media beat my door down, when the world was my oyster, when perhaps you've heard? I was Fired.

Certainly, my Firing does not feel Cinderella-like at its outset. Monday morning my public radio station manager phones me apoplectic. She says I said "fuck" on the radio! How could I do such a destructive thing! I've endangered the entire station! She has no choice but to fire me immediately and, "Please Sandra," she finishes, "get some help. Get . . . professional . . . help. Good-bye." Dial tone. The horror begins.

The horror is that clearly a mistake has been made. In my short commentary praising a recent Bette Midler concert, in a sly tribute, I thought, to her blueness I had recorded a throwaway expletive which, as we'd done for the past six years, the engineer was supposed to humorously bleep. He clearly forgot and the "fuck" has since aired, not once but twice it turns out! Because when my commentary ran at my new, supposedly plum time slot of 7:25 A.M. Sunday morning, no one in the entire city caught it! So it went gaily on to run a second time at 9:25, like the little "fuck" that could. Okay, I think—at lunch with my sister, who is paying—on the positive side, the pay was a hundred fifty bucks a week, so it's no financial tragedy. But now what's hitting me is humiliation, the sheer raw humiliation of being fired at forty-two. Forty-two!

Still MacArthur genius grant–free, the first gentle waves of the forties pooling around my ankles. Sure, I've made the best of the bones tossed my way, writing literary funny bits for my public radio station's endless pledge drives, teaching felons, putting a brave face on ever-worsening health insurance, "A co-payment of a hundred five dollars? I guess that's not bad." For those of us who don't peak at twenty-five, our career trajectories are a wonderful gradual maturing, a mellowing, a kind of goldening, I like to think.

In your twenties you're promising; thirties, honing; and by forty, you're secure in the knowledge that if you're not rich, at least in your own small way you're a . . . treasure, a cultural treasure. But no. According to my boss, it's "You said 'fuck' on the radio. Fuck you!"

"Amy Tan's career—that's the one I really wanted!" I snarl, sloshing my wine, bitter. "It's like I'm not even part of the NPR cosmos anymore, I'm excommunicated! There's Andrei Codrescu, Bailey White, and this stinking hole where my gentle musings used to be. 'Get professional help!' She's the crazy one! She's famous for it!"

How many are we, the fired people, who enter boozy spirals, shaking our fists, fantasizing that our firing is so unfair it will trigger outrage, national public outrage! When word hits the streets, we think, searing op-eds should be penned, mobs should form, phone systems should be shut down by avalanches of angry calls!

Well, for once this actually happens. My firing turns into an eleventh-hour Cinderella story. My unlikely fairy godmother?

Janet Jackson's boob. Which is to say that while I myself am nationally obscure, my firing occurs just weeks after the Super Bowl, during an election year. The media is obsessed with obscenity, and an obsentity firing is big news! News bulletins start bubbling in: "Fired for obscenity, Howard Stern, Bubba the Love Sponge, and . . . Sandra Tsing Loh? Who the fuck is she?"

My little "fuck" that could just gains more and more steam. It starts making the *Drudge Report*, the *Nation*, *Variety*, *Rolling Stone*, the *New York Times*, Reuters, the BBC. By the weekend it's in the crawl under Larry King: "Radio commentator Sandra Tsing Loh fired for obscenity!" My friends are reading about it! "Sandra Tsing Loh! Fired! Obscene!"

Overnight I'm transformed from a minivan-driving mother of two into a rockin' First Amendment heroine, free speech pioneer, modern-day Lenny Bruce! Which brings in the big guys: Bill Maher! George Carlin! Howard Stern rails about my case for an hour! "Even little public radio knitting ladies are gettin' fired! Fuck the FCC! Fuck!" True, I'd actually been in the middle of a five-part series on knitting. Point is, the shooting media star of my obscenity takes on a glamour, a cultural heat my actual employment never has! NBC casting calls, they want me to read for the part of Jeff Goldblum's therapist! Depressed artist friends are calling: "I wish I could get fired. You're so lucky. I wish I could get a career break like that."

It all drives my station manager nuts! "Like I said, Sandra is an emotionally unstable person who tried to pull a Janet Jackson." In the *L.A. Times* every single day it's she says, I say, she says, I say. A kind of wild, over-the-top *Mothra Versus Godzilla* battle! People are fascinated because they've never seen anything like this in public radio. This is like Jerry Springer, but the NPR version, with two haggard women in flat-heeled shoes hitting each other over the head with 100 percent recycled material tote bags and pledge drive coffee mugs. "And here—a Yo-Yo Ma CD! Bill Frisell! And what's this? The Kronos Quartet doing the songs of Elvis Costello!"

Then, like uncaged animals, here come the listeners. Phoning and writing in outrage! Because my boss called my firing a "preemptive distancing." "She's the Marge Schott of public radio!" one screams. They've gone nuts, these subscribers. It's like a middle-class riot! They're saying they're going to stand and boo the station's trailers in independent movie theaters! They're sending old pledge tote bags to the station, filled with years of membership cards, all cut up! They're saying, "We're very disappointed. Instead of our usual hundred dollars a year? We're contemplating just giving . . . twenty-five." Ouch! And the F-bomb? Now that it's been uttered on public radio, it's like people are liberated. They can't stop saying it! Sample e-mail, and I quote: "Sandra: I fucking find it fucking outrageous that you should have been summarily fucking fired for having inadvertently used a 'naughty' fucking word on the fucking air. To my mind, it's part and parcel of the Massive Wave of Fucking Stupidity that seems, once again, to be washing over this fucking country. FUCK! Just because fucking Middle America saw a black woman's tit during a fucking football game. Who gives a fuck?"

What I finally ended up saying to the press, in the words of another accidental L.A. icon, was, "Please, can't we all just get along?" And it turns out we could, she on her side of town, and me on the other, at my new public radio station. Living happily ever after.

Sandra Tsing Loh is the author of *A Year in Van Nuys* and *Depth Takes a Holiday.* She has a big and loyal fan base that has followed her weekly show, *The Loh Life,* to its new location on *Marketplace* on American Public Radio.

FIRED FACT

Psychologists surveyed nine hundred working women to measure their happiness while interacting with different people. On a scale of 0 to 4, only being in their bosses' company was less desirable than being alone.[1]

INTERACTING WITH	AVERAGE HAPPINESS
friends	3.7
family	3.4
clients	2.8
alone	2.7
the boss	2.4

EXTRA! EXTRA!

Brian Unger

I was fired for how I look. Never, ever in my wildest dreams did I think it would happen to me, that I would share anything with Margaret Cho. She was fired from TV for how she looks too . . . then published her story in a book. I could never do that.

Every day in Hollywood people don't get jobs because of how they look or for having the wrong look. These people just look wrong. And for being wrong-looking, they are jobless and poor. But once in a while, a freak mutation occurs in Hollywood's genetic code, and a wrong-looking person slips right through. They get a job . . . until they're caught for not looking right. Because eventually someone says, "Something doesn't look right about this. I'm afraid we've hired the wrong look."

Anyway, on my first day as the host of a popular entertainment news show—we'll call it *Extra*, because that's what it's called—I received a handwritten note from my boss. It read, "Today we start the adventure of a lifetime, as we remake the show . . ." In my image, presumably. Yes, a team of professionals was going to tailor a viewing experience to my look. The show would be reconstructed to look like me. I would look like the show. We would look at each other and say, "You're Brian Unger!" "No, I'm the show." We would complete each other. Adventure of a lifetime, hello!

I always thought an adventure of a lifetime would be becoming a father, surfing Pipeline, or meeting a beautiful woman in a Paris café, spending hours Bush bashing, sampling wines, and agreeing to meet exactly six months later. We consummate our budding relationship and slip into sleep still holding each other in our arms; I wake up in a bathtub filled with ice in a dark brothel in Prague missing my kidneys. No, no, an adventure of a lifetime is hosting *Extra*.

The note went on: "Feel free to leave your imprint everywhere!" Wow. Not only would this show be an extension of me and my look, I could shit all over it, freely! With impunity. I had permission to lift my leg and leave my essence *everywhere*. On everyone and everything. People would walk around saying to each other, "Oh my God, you've been marked by Brian Unger! I smell his seed all over you!"

Hey, that's what the note said. Or at least that's how I read it.

For all this adventurous imprinting, I would be paid $500,000 a year. It's not Topher Grace money. But this was more money than I had ever been paid to leave my imprint everywhere *and* merely act interested in the Jennifers. I asked Jennifer Lopez when she planned to get married. For that money, I asked Jennifer Garner who she was wearing. I even asked Jennifer Aniston, "Why are most rapes committed by people we know? Why isn't that message getting through!" It was like stealing money!

Other than an overwhelming feeling that I was living a lie, things went well for two months. Ratings climbed 16 percent. And besides getting to talk to Jennifer Aniston about rape, I got a chance to ask a hero of mine, Keanu Reeves, in a whimsical moment, if there would ever be a sequel to *Point Break*. He didn't know. In fact he just stared at me weirdly and said, "I really don't remember the movie."

That's when things began to change. I started hearing there was something not right about my look. At first the note from upstairs was subtle: "No more sweaters, if he wants to keep his job." It was as if I were a stripper who wasn't showing enough ass.

And so my wardrobe became suits, dark ones, mostly black. And gradually, day by day, I began looking more and more like a young Romanian Johnny Cash. And I started feeling self-conscious and asked the wardrobe stylist things like "Why do I match the scenery?" Which she somehow heard as "Brian wants to fuck me!"

Then, from upstairs another note: Something was wrong with my makeup. So the makeup artist—a wonderful man whom I thought of as a doting aunt—was ordered to paint large white circles under my eyes that made me appear like a terrified raccoon on the set. This, I'm told, is "concealer." Concealing my membership in the human species and turning me into a rodent!

In a dangerous chain reaction, my look began wasting away, devouring itself like a planeload of soccer players stranded in the Andes. Word came down again. This time—my hair. It was just wrong hair. Translation: Cut it, color it, blow it dry, then recut it, recolor it, and blow it dry again. Fire hairstylist. Repeat.

When it was all done—the new suit, new face, and new hair—I was now John Tesh. A shiny, waxy man, the kind I'd sat-irized for most of my career. I had become my own punch line.

And yet there remained one last thing to change—my imme-diate presence.

I received a memo detailing this matter: "Dear Brian, I know this is a confusing time for you. Let me try to clear things up a bit. Our set is lit for a solo blond anchor. For that reason, every time we go to you on our set, the shot isn't flattering. You look too pale or your eyes look half closed and the shot makes your nose look twice as big. It's a distorted image. You also come off as having low energy and like you're not having any fun. So, the immediate plan is to have you field anchor from Hollywood and Highland. I'm working on having better cameras moved to the studio. Thanks for being such a trouper."

Now, I'd heard of people "breaking cameras" before—as a joke, like "With a face like that, you're gonna break the camera!" But no one had ever written it to me in a memo, attacking my nose and my sense of "fun." And for understanding this, I was a trouper.

So, I was moved—from the studio to an outdoor mall at the height of the rainy season in Los Angeles.

Like a dog that wasn't housebroken, I was kept outdoors for two months, miles away, at Hollywood and Highland, home of the Oscars and the Sunglass Hut. Each morning I was driven there by a producer and told to stand in the rain and read a script that began, "And right here in Hollywood . . ." as a few Latino gangbangers watched. Oddly, my nose remained the same size, and my fun factor . . .

Do you recall the final scene from *The Elephant Man*, when the grotesquely disfigured fellow finally rests his head on a pillow? I put my head down too, but it landed on my computer keyboard, hitting the "forward nose & fun memo to attorney" key. At last, peace.

On the Friday before Christmas, I was officially released. I said good-bye to no one at *Extra*—not to wardrobe, makeup, or my team of hairstylists. I just walked to the door, turned to the other inmates, and said, "I'll tell the world about you."

The commandant who ran the stalag called *Extra* had one thing right about me: "It was a distorted image." Yes, I was hired for how I looked, but over time it couldn't compete with how I saw myself. I can finally say, Keanu, you are a moron.

Brian Unger is a writer/comedian living in L.A. He is a weekly commentator on NPR's *Day to Day* and a former correspondent and producer on *The Daily Show.* He hasn't been near a red carpet in two years.

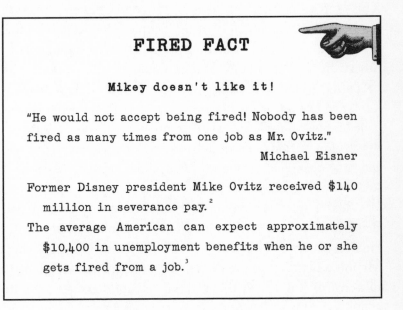

FIRED FACT

Mikey doesn't like it!

"He would not accept being fired! Nobody has been fired as many times from one job as Mr. Ovitz."

Michael Eisner

Former Disney president Mike Ovitz received $140 million in severance pay.[2]

The average American can expect approximately $10,400 in unemployment benefits when he or she gets fired from a job.[3]

SCHADENFREUDE

Anne Meara

This topic—getting fired—should come under the title Schadenfreude, since most of the people interviewed for this book have triumphed over their humiliating consignments to Siberia by the very nature of their comparative success in life, or if not in life, then in their chosen professions. I think *success* is a relative term. I had a cousin who suffered from what is now called bipolar illness. She had extreme highs and lows, and during the low periods she could barely get out of bed. So one day she had an epiphany, got out of bed, and washed her face. This was, in my estimation, success.

When I was a freshman in high school, my dearest pal, Patsy-Jo Shannon, got me an afterschool job working in the kitchen of Mercy Hospital in Rockville Centre, Long Island. My job was to set up the dinner trays for the patients (mostly obstetrical) and deliver them to the new mothers. At the time a musical film called *State Fair*, starring Dick Haymes and Jeanne Crain, was playing locally, and Patsy-Jo and I loved it so much we saw it twice. Everywhere I went I would sing the hit song from the movie, "It Isn't Even Spring." At least I think that's the title. Singing is not what I do best, but in my mind, especially after some chardonnay enhancement, I'm Donna Murphy.

I really enjoyed setting up the trays and belting out "It Isn't Even Spring." The kitchen staff loved it. They laughed. I was a hit with this captive audience (they had to work there, not me, I was a part-time candy striper). Drunk with power, I continued singing as I made my rounds through the hospital corridors.

The head nurse happened to be a nun. In fact most of the nurses were nuns since this was a Catholic hospital. Sister Mary Vicious sprang out of nowhere, a black and white apparition with the speed of a storm trooper on patrol in WW II. She relieved me of my food cart and bellowed at me, "You're a disgrace. Leave the premises immediately!"

People in the hallway looked at me pityingly as I walked the walk of shame back to the kitchen. This was my second day on the job and I was washed up.

Years later, after graduating from medical school and completing my internship, I started a successful practice in obstetrics. On one occasion I was performing a particularly complicated C-section at the very same hospital where I had suffered my humiliation. Irony of ironies, my assisting nurse happened to be, you guessed it, Sister Mary Vicious. She was totally inept in the delivery room and almost dropped the baby, which I retrieved just in the nick of time. I told her to leave immediately. Later out in the hallway I saw this mass of black and white crumpled in a heap on the floor, whimpering. I approached Sister Mary Vicious, helped her up, and confronted her.

"Sister, don't you recognize me? I was the teenager you fired from this very hospital all those years ago." Her face scrunched into a mask of sobs. "Oh, God forgive me, Dr. Meara, I was so wrong. Forgive me, forgive me," she wailed. Eventually I did forgive her, but those hurts die hard. When I visit her every now and then in the old nuns' home, her withered face lights up with joy and I realize the lessons of compassion and forgiveness she taught me.

Hey, I'm just playin' with you. The first part is true, the last part is bogus. Actually I never did see Sister Mary Vicious again. And my doctorate was in quantum physics, not obstetrics.

Anne Meara never pursued the medical profession but does frequent astrophysics Web sites. She is one-half of the venerated comedy team Stiller and Meara and an award-winning actress and playwright.

FIRED FACT

In 1781 Wolfgang Amadeus Mozart visited Vienna in the company of his employer, the harsh Hieronymous Graf Von Colloredo, and fell out with him. According to Mozart's own testimony, he was dismissed literally "with a kick in the seat of the pants." The Prince fired him declaring, *"Mag Er geh'n, Ich brauch' Ihn nicht!"* ("May he leave, I'll miss him not!") [4]

SENT TO CYBERIA

Lori Gottlieb

When I signed on with a high-profile Internet startup in the spring of 2000, I couldn't believe my good fortune. The gig came with a VP title, 70,000 stock options (pre-IPO, of course), and the promise of "empowering the teen girl generation." Three months later, though, I walked out with nothing but an overwhelming sense of disillusionment, a box of glitter nail polish, and a video entitled *An Intimate Guide to Male Genital Massage*.

I had just published a book based on my teen diaries when I was recruited by the CEO of a startup described as a "digital hangout" for teen girls. Each of the Web site's so-called channels—ranging from Wellness to Beauty to Adventure—would be run by an adult mentor/guide, called a "Face" (there was a Face of Wellness and a Face of Adventure, for example), who the CEO said was "a cross between a big sister and an MTV veejay." The Faces would write smart, inspiring content and interact with teen girls in cyberspace.

The company was called Kibu, which meant something like "foundation." In Japanese. So what if it was a name that no one in America could pronounce or even clearly define? I happily jumped aboard the dot-com bus.

Month 1: Warning Signs
Even before I started the job, there were clues that my bus might have some mechanical problems.

- Although I was hired to be in charge of content for the entire site, Kibu didn't check my references before offering me the job. Not one. Nor had they checked the references of the fifty-plus employees already on staff. Which I guess made sense if you consider that the trendy twentysomethings paid lawyerlike salaries to produce and write content for their channels had worked in completely unrelated jobs—a hairstylist, a Saks counter makeup artist, and a former fashion model. I mean, whom could they call for a reference, Eileen Ford?

- I was joining a company in which twenty of the people reporting directly to me were called "Faces," and one in particular was called the Face of Hair.
- Mere moments after I was told during my interview that the CEO's management style was about "totally open communication," I was asked to keep information that a current editor was leaving a secret.

Despite these ominous signs, I gushed to friends about how I couldn't wait to start my exotic new job. Sounds crazy, I know, but I can explain it in two words: Jim Jones. It was like everyone in the dot-com world had imbibed from the same keg of Kool-Aid. And I was willing to drink the sickly sweet punch not only because everyone else was but, frankly, because these people seemed to be doing well. Very well. They drove $60,000 cars. They thought nothing of spending $20 on lunch each day. Our CEO had started a company that was sold to Mattel for $26 million. Our investors included former Netscape guru Jim Clark and the most prestigious backer of all, the legendary venture capital firm Kleiner Perkins Caufield & Byers.

Who was I to question their wisdom?

So I didn't panic when, my first day on the job, I learned that Kibu's business model was nothing more than a string of nifty-sounding phrases like "online integrated marketing." According to our CEO, this had something to do with girls' getting redeemable points for responding to surveys furnished by our sponsors. Never mind that we had neither sponsors nor an audience of teen girls.

Apparently we would make money through e-commerce. The only problem was, we didn't have any products to sell. As far as I could tell, the only thing Kibu actually produced—and quite successfully, thanks to our savvy publicist—was an avalanche of splashy press releases promising both a unique Web community and a revenue stream that didn't exist. It was genius: the PR blitz spawned dozens of fawning articles. And we began to believe our own hype. In fact, we became our own biggest fans.

Which is why I still wasn't particularly worried when on my second day the weekly companywide meeting consisted of singing "Happy Birthday" (no one broke thirty), complimenting a staffer on her "hot" red leather pants, sharing "your most embarrassing story" (most had something to do with wraparound skirts falling off at inopportune times), and, for no apparent reason (no deal closed, no significant jump in teen girl subscribers), applauding ourselves for how great we were. No matter what someone said ("It's Tuesday"; "That's Shannon's sushi"), it was always followed by a cacophony of high-pitched whistles and applause. This was our company "culture." And according to our CEO, the Kibu culture was as important as the product. As a result, we accomplished nothing at these weekly meetings, but boy, did we love ourselves.

So I was especially surprised that the editorial meeting I called the next day turned out to be not another chummy lovefest but the most frustrating meeting I'd ever run—and this includes the time I volunteered to lead a group of troubled teens in prison. After some witty introductory remarks, I handed out proposed deadlines and production schedules for each channel, which were met not with cheers or applause but with dead silence and blank stares. The only noise in the room came from a dropped metal hair clip that the Face of Hair was using to style the Face of Books's hair.

Finally the Face of School (whose sole qualification for this job seemed to be that she'd once gone to school herself—albeit as a self-described C student) asked, "What does an editor do?" I explained that I would help the Faces brainstorm, generate ideas, and refine their pieces, but it soon became apparent that the Faces thought I'd be writing their copy for them. Tears were shed. Voices were raised. Whines resounded. So much for Kibu culture.

To calm everybody down, I decided to meet with each Face one-on-one to address their concerns and offer some guidance. First, however, I needed to check in with our CEO, who had preemptively declared that she didn't like to get "bogged down with details." I gave her the big picture: We didn't yet have the budget, manpower, or sponsors to support twenty channels. I suggested eventually consolidating some channels, like folding Advice into Relationships, and discarding others that seemed doomed to unprofitability, like Animals (most seventeen-year-old girls are more interested in penises than in panda stickers).

That meant some Faces would have to be fired. "Okay, you can let them go," the CEO replied. "Now?" I asked. I mentioned that maybe she should be the one to do that since I'd literally just met these people and I hadn't been the one to hire them. But she was adamant that I wield the ax.

"And they're not being fired," she corrected me. "They're being unhired."

Apparently, firing was also bad for the Kibu culture.

The Face of Animals took her unhiring gracefully (she had a day job at the local zoo), but the Face of Advice, a psychology intern, immediately burst into tears. This was followed by pleading ("The girls need me!"), hysteria (hiccupy sobbing), threats ("I want my image taken off the site immediately!"), and, although I'm no therapist, what seemed like suicidal ideation ("This job meant everything to me! It was my life!"). To make matters worse, I had to cancel the Face of Advice's upcoming story, "How to Deal with Rejection."

A few days later I called her to tie up some loose ends and see how she was doing. "I still can't believe I'm being fired!" she wailed.

"Oh, no," I assured her. "You're not being fired. You're just being, you know, unhired." It didn't sound that strange at the time.

The Kool-Aid's buzz really began to wear off after I met with the remaining Faces to discuss their respective channels. Over the next few weeks I learned that the Face of Horoscopes didn't "believe in astrology"; the Face of Fashion, who drove a Porsche and had a condo in Hawaii, kept forgetting that teen girls shop at the Gap, not Gucci; the Face of Beauty used the word *luscious* so incessantly (luscious lipstick, luscious liner, luscious lids) that when I did a search for *luscious* and left "replace with" blank, the word count in her 150-word column went down by 30; and the Face of Guys, a Backstreet Boys lookalike and the Face of Hair's nineteen-year-old brother, thought I was being unreasonable because I wouldn't let him wax poetic about his favorite men's magazine, *Maxim*, on a site that was supposed to provide "insight" and "inspiration" to teen girls.

Something had to change.

Month 2: Silicon Valley 90210

Apparently our CEO needed a change too. At the weekly staff meeting she announced that, in the interest of preventing burnout, she was heading to a beach in Hawaii. By coincidence our cofounder (a former secretary and sorority girl) was already in Hawaii, as was our Face of Fashion. At a later staff meeting we were treated to photos of the three perched on stools at a ritzy hotel's beachfront bar, laughing with a beefy pro football player and sipping giant mimosas.

With our bosses bronzing, I worked eighty-hour weeks, broke out in stress acne, stopped exercising, wore only sweatpants, and let my curly hair air-dry as I returned an onslaught of calls on the way to work each morning. Meantime everyone else at Kibu looked like they'd just stepped off the set of *Beverly Hills 90210* or *Dawson's Creek*. They dutifully coaxed any unseemly frizzy hair into glossy, straight tresses like Katie Holmes's. They all dressed the same (tight Lycra tops, capris, wedgy sandals), acted the same (kiss-kiss, rah-rah enthusiastic), spoke the same ("Rockin'!" "Right on!" "You go, girl!" "*Love* it!"), and had the same interests (boyfriends, the perfect G-string).

Suddenly it hit me: Kibu had become the world of its target audience. In high school you were either cool or you were not, and if there's one thing I learned from being a teenager, it was that if you wanted to exert any power, you had to be in the popular crowd.

There was only one thing to do: I called an emergency meeting with the Face of Hair.

The effects of the flat iron, a hair-straightening device that allowed me to look like the rest of my Kibu kin, were instantaneous. The Faces complimented me on my sleek locks. They said hi to me in the cafeteria and invited me to parties. They slipped me eye shadow and blush samples as tokens of our truce. They even confided their boyfriend and imaginary cellulite problems by the latte machine. When I started dating someone new, the Face of Relationships gave me a "highly recommended" instructional video, a hand-job bacchanal narrated by two unbelievably well-endowed hotties that had been circulating in the office: *An Intimate Guide to Male Genital Massage.* Most important, the Faces actually showed up for most of their story meetings, appreciated my suggestions, and turned in their work pretty close to deadline. I was beginning to think that there might be hope for Kibu after all.

Until, that is, the CEO returned from Hawaii. Although the Faces were doing their best, Kibu still needed a major overhaul. The site needed a better design, and half the time it broke down. Besides, we still weren't making money because nobody could decide which buzzword Kibu was: was it a community, a destination, a portal, a multimedia enterprise, or a digital lifestyle brand?

When I raised these issues with our CEO, her response was to label me as "negative." If there was one thing she couldn't abide, it was people who weren't "team players." Kibu had to be a place of fun and happiness, and that took priority.

That night I went home and, instead of editing, watched the male genital massage video with my boyfriend. When the narrator kept referring to a ten-foot-high replica of the male genital organ as a "magic wand," I remarked to my boyfriend that unless Kibu's management did a reality check—and fast—it would take a real magic wand to make the company viable.

Month 3: The emperor's new clothes

At our next staff meeting two men, purportedly there to "observe," appeared at the conference table. One was Kibu's first (not to mention belated) VP of finance and the other was one of our investors (who kept glancing at his watch and didn't seem amused by our "most embarrassing story" ritual).

Although "girls who get it" was Kibu's slogan, it seemed that these two male outsiders might be the ones truly "getting it." Our new VP of finance convinced our CEO that things like, say, budgets needed to go into effect immediately. Employees had to account for their time and meet deadlines. I was to come up with an editorial plan for the company. Kibu was in crisis mode, but at least our energy was being focused in the right direction.

And then, astonishingly, our CEO eloped. To Bali. Upon her return, I got an e-mail asking if I could meet with her. I felt optimistic: I assumed she wanted to discuss the changes I had outlined while she was away. But when I walked into the conference room, I learned that this was "a termination discussion," which meant that I was being "unhired." Apparently I'd violated the most important rule of the dot-com world: I'd said, out loud and in earnest, that the emperor had no clothes.

I wasn't surprised when my dot-com bus sputtered and ran out of gas after just five months of operation. But two months before, on that fateful day when I was escorted out by security (but not before confiscating some glitter nail polish and the hand-job video), I went home shell-shocked. For the first week I sat by my phone like a rejected girlfriend, hoping that the CEO would call and un-unhire me. Later though, sipping my Kibu-branded chai energy tea, I reflected on all that I'd learned from my brief startup experience: Trust your instincts, not the drunken herd. Don't place your bets on buzzwords. If you jump on a bus, make sure you know its destination. And finally, when it comes to male genital massage, always err on the side of too much oil.

Lori Gottlieb is a commentator on NPR's *All Things Considered*. She no longer flat-irons her hair but she is the author of several books, including *Stick Figure*.

FIRED FACT

Ratio between the pay received by the average American CEO and the average American worker in 2004: 431 to 1. In 1980 it was 42 to 1.

Ratio between the pay received by the average Japanese CEO and the average Japanese worker in 2004: 10 to 1.[5]

HARRY SHEARER MINDS
HIS CREDIBILITY GAP

In radio, being fired is a way of life. I've been fired three times on the radio. The first time, I had a show on a station in L.A. that also carried an insanely popular show called *The Feminine Forum*. The host would talk about sex to housewives and was always coming on to them with elaborate euphemisms, like "Won't you stroke my stallion ganglia."[6] So on my show I decided to break it down and I replaced all his euphemisms with "penis." I got a call from the station manager, who fired me, saying, "You can't say 'penis' on the radio! I can understand 'shit' or 'fuck,' but why would you say 'penis'?"

The second time I was fired, it was for playing Mel Tormé on a rock station.

My third time was a group firing. Michael McKean, Richard Beebe, David Lander, and I had a comedy group called the Credibility Gap. Our station's program director, Johnny Darin, also had a show; his tag line was "in with Dar-in crowd." Perhaps he was jealous because we got so much more mail than he did. In any event, he canceled the show. He told us we were going to do the straight news show and each news segment would be called "the something gap."

Well, we couldn't quit 'cause we wanted the unemployment money so we had to get fired. Richard read the news at a depressingly slow pace; you just wanted to kill yourself listening to it. I did a bad Paul Harvey imitation—pauses for no reason, no punch lines, stories that would go nowhere, just trail off. After a week we were fired. Last time I saw Johnny, he was reading the stock quotes on channel 22.

Actually, we got fired another time. The Credibility Gap moved to a new station, but this time, to avoid getting involved in station politics, we were working in a studio off-site. Well, the word had gotten around that everyone at the station was going to be fired and the deejays had locked themselves in the studio and were on the radio inviting people to come on down to the station to see them get fired. Eventually the manager came in and fired them on the air. One of the deejays said, "Hey, what about the Credibility Gap?" We heard the manager say—and this is on the air, mind you—"They're fired too." I'll never forget what he said to me when we came in to get our checks. He said, "I envy you your freedom."

As a writer I've had the please-fire-me experience. Comedian Tom Leopold and I were hired to do a rewrite of a movie called *Club Paradise*. Only two words of what we wrote actually appeared in the movie, the title: *Club Paradise*. I was so appalled by the movie, I wanted to use a pseudonym for my credit, and I suggested to the producer Michael Shamberg that the name I wanted to use was Jeremy Shamberg so it would look like the writer had been hired because of nepotism. It was arbitrated by the Writers' Guild, and I lost the case, so the credit I settled on was Ed Roboto.

I was also fired twice from *Saturday Night Live*. I came on in Lorne Michael's last year of his first tenure on the show, and when he left, Jean Doumanian came in to run the show. Everyone else had left the show, and I met with Jean and offered to stay on. I told her I thought it was important that she bring on experienced people. She said, "Honestly, I don't think I want people who know what they are doing." That was that. Then after *This Is Spinal Tap* came out, they wooed Chris Guest, Martin Short, and me to come back to the show. I was really unhappy. At 1:43 A.M. on Jan 13, 1985, Dick Ebersole said to me, "This isn't working out. Why don't you just go?" I said, "I'd be delighted but you're going to pay me for the rest of the year."

The next day the show announced in the trades that I had left because of "creative differences." So the *New York Times* called me, and this is the kind of thing you could never think of if you had planned it. They asked if I had left because of creative differences, and I said, "Yes, I was creative and they were different."

Harry Shearer received an Emmy nomination for his ill-fated tenure on *SNL* and is now the host of *Le Show,* a weekly radio show on NPR from which he has never been fired. He is best known for his roles in *This Is Spinal Tap, Best in Show, A Mighty Wind,* and the characters he voices on *The Simpsons,* including Homer Simpson's boss, Mr. Burns.

FIRED FACT

Hey, where'd my job go? You might be asking yourself that if you work for any of these companies: Delphi would like to give more free time to 18,000 workers, Merck saying aloha to 7,000, Ford waving so long to 30,000, GM throwing 30,000 overboard, Kimberly-Clark giving the old heave-ho to 6,000, Sony saying bon voyage to 20,000, Kodak wishing 22,000 workers a lot of luck out there.[7]

FIRED BY THE QUEEN AND DUMPED BY TRUMP

Joyce Beber

"Be sure to look at *her* when you present. He may be the biggest real estate developer in New York, but *she* calls the shots." That was the sage advice her friendly real-estate woman gave me as I prepared for my first audience.

The "she" was Leona Helmsley. I had been summoned to the Palm Beach penthouse of Mr. and Mrs. Harry Helmsley on a Sunday afternoon to present my advertising agency's credentials. We had been recommended to them as a capable and creative shop that could handle advertising for a new hotel they were building in New York City overlooking the spires of Saint Patrick's Cathedral and aptly named the Palace.

I did as I was told. I politely acknowledged the tall, regal Harry, but I remembered Disraeli's advice about how to talk to Queen Victoria: "When it comes to flattery, lay it on with a trowel." I did just that. In the middle of my pitch, after I complimented Leona on her perspicacity in recognizing the intention of a particular advertisement for the third time, she snuggled up to the visibly bored Harry seated next to her on the couch and said, "Hire her." We were in. My Miami-based advertising agency, Beber Silverstein, was hired to introduce the Palace, and in the process we conceived an advertising campaign that anointed a queen. Though she had greeted me herself in bare feet and shorts, her bejeweled and imperious demeanor told a more complete story.

We were entering the material '80s, and working for Leona, the ultimate Material Girl, was nothing if not exciting. She was the glamorous diva with the fabulous furs, the gravelly voice, and the potty mouth. Long before bling-bling was fashion, she had Marilyn Monroe's notion about diamonds: the bigger the better.

Every year she threw her low-key, Quaker husband a spectacular themed formal dinner dance on his birthday. If Harry was king, she was the magnificently dressed queen, complete with diamond tiara borrowed for the occasion from Harry Winston's. Leona would sweep into the ballroom on Harry's arm as the twenty-two-piece orchestra played "I'm Just Wild about Harry and Harry's Wild about Lee." It was their theme song, and watching them dance together with perfect ballroom ease, for a moment you had to put down your beluga caviar and believe.

"Fall in love again," she whispered into my ear as she floated by in her strapless white lace, crystal-encrusted ball gown and patted my husband Chuck's head.

"Nowadays, everyone wants to be a star," Frank Sinatra cracked to Laurance Rockefeller as he watched the happy couple sail past their table.

Barbara Walters, Walter Cronkite, Mike Wallace, the governor of New York, real estate tycoons, and Hollywood celebrities—they were all there. I could get used to this, and I did.

"I need an ad director. I don't have time for this. Hire me one." It was a royal command and I obeyed by hiring an out-of-work friend of a good friend who, we were told, would make a loyal employee. Just a few months later our handpicked ad director convinced Leona that he could save her 15 percent of her advertising budget.

"I can do just as good a job in-house," he explained.

"Good," she agreed.

"Sorry," said our ex-friend. "Business is business."

"You're fired," Leona said.

Being fired was only the beginning. More painful was her refusal to pay outstanding obligations. Monies owed to *The New Yorker, Travel & Leisure*, the *New York Times*, and a host of airline magazines was withheld.

"Sue me," Leona said when we called begging to be paid.

So we did. My partner Elaine Silverstein traveled back and forth to New York to meet with lawyers. On the day before the trial, we settled for what we were owed. Which meant, of course, we were out the lawyers' fees.

A few weeks later I received a call from Leona. I suspected the ad director would be in over his head. Indeed, he had been fired. She seduced us by offering a free suite at her Palace: offices from which we could handle our New York accounts, like Coty Perfumes, Steinway Pianos, and Lalique.

For the next ten years we had a wonderful time making her even more glamorous in a series of ads, not only for the Helmsley Palace but for her other New York hotels as well. People quoted her headlines: "I wouldn't settle for skimpy towels. Why should you?" The advertising campaign was taught on college campuses to illustrate effective advertising. Leona Helmsley was an icon. She was also the darling of the female impersonators, right up there with Judy Garland, Barbra Streisand, and Bette Midler.

Then one day the phone in the Miami office rang. "You stole from me," Leona screamed into the receiver. "I know you're against me. I never want to see your ugly puss again. I heard you're working for Donald Trump. Don't come back here. I'm evicting you. You're fired."

In fact we weren't working for Trump, not yet, but when the queen made up her mind about something, reality was of little concern. We were sacked for a second time. Again we were not paid. Again we had a raft of magazines clamoring for payment. Again we had to hire legal representation, more costly this time, as we had that extra little complication of the landlord issue. Again there were depositions. Again we settled at the eleventh hour.

On a trip to New York for one such meeting, I was trapped with her in the same elevator. She looked me in the eye, stuck her finger down her throat, and gagged. We did not know that her legal maneuvers with us were just a skirmish for Leona. She was preparing for a much more serious battle, one that would land her in the pokey for tax evasion. No wonder she was out of sorts.

Six months after her release from prison, where Leona had spent eighteen months (reduced from four years for good behavior), I received a call from her male secretary. Marty was back. It was his third or fourth reprise in twenty years.

"Would you consider coming back?" he asked. "*I* did."

"I don't know, Marty."

"You should at least hear what she has to say," he said. "She needs you. Come with Elaine. It's beautiful out here."

"Out here?"

"We're in Scottsdale."

"I'll think about it." I went in to talk to Elaine. "How would you like to go to the Biltmore in Scottsdale for a couple of days?"

"The Biltmore? Frank Lloyd Wright's Biltmore?"

"Yep."

"Sure I would."

"Good. We're going on Saturday."

"What for?" Elaine asked.

"To see Leona. Just a meeting."

Elaine threw up all the way to Arizona. I told her it was a twenty-four-hour virus. She said she had come down with Leonitis.

A driver picked us up and drove us through three sets of security gates to a lone house that sat on the top of a mountain. Leona opened the door in bare feet just as she had when I first met her in Palm Beach. The house was enormous. She took us to see Harry. He sat immaculate and impassive in a wheelchair. She chatted and charmed. He was silent, no longer able to speak. When lunch was served, he was wheeled to his place at the table. His lunch was fed to him by a male attendant, spoon by spoon. I thought of the days when the elegant Harry had stood on their balcony, taking in the sweeping view of Manhattan. "Just taking inventory," he would kid.

"I'd like to do a comeback campaign," she explained. "They're ruining my business. There hasn't been any advertising in three years. You'd like that, wouldn't you, Harry?" she said to the mute, reduced man seated in his chair. "See?" she said. "He just blinked yes. He always blinks with his eyes."

As a convicted felon, Leona could no longer be the queen. All we had to do was find a way to sell her hotels without using her name. We came up with a campaign that relied on the basic principle that always produces the best advertising: State the irrefutable truth. "Say what you will, she runs a helluva hotel." It worked. "She" was back.

Harry died a few years later. Leona traveled from one of her empty mansions to another. I invited the always-lonely Leona to my home in Miami. On one such occasion we were both asked to attend a small, elegant dinner party given by a banker friend. There she and I both met, and she was captivated by, a forty-five-year-old optometrist. She promptly hired him to run her hotels. Experience wasn't necessary. She wanted him around. She fantasized a grand romance. It might be May and December, but she was a young eighty. He took her to the art museums. He bought her violets for her furs. He sent her love notes. But one fateful day someone in her organization, fearful of the man's growing control over Leona, outed him. He was toast.

She was on the phone once again. "You set me up," a heartsick and enraged Leona shrieked. "This is your fault. You did this to me. You fixed me up with a fairy."

"But," I protested, "we both met him the same night."

"I don't care," she bellowed. "I thought you were my friend. You're fired."

Once more we were out the door, going through the same painful drill to get monies owed the agency. Once burned, twice learned, and the third time . . . I asked myself why I kept setting myself up for further humiliation. But in my business, if you're not getting fired, you're not really in the game. Being tough and resilient isn't just an asset, it's a requirement. During a downturn in the economy and a rough passage in our business, our agency softball team wore T-shirts that read, "We've lost more than you'll ever bill." But to be hired and fired and left unpaid three times by the same person? I guess I could rationalize and say that an ad agency run by two middle-aged doctor's wives competing with the big boys needed every showcase account it could get. The truth was I loved the Palace intrigue. Leona captivated me. She could be absolutely charming when it suited her. I liked her verve and her humor. She was fun to be around. Mrs. H. could personally nurse your cold with homemade chicken soup on Wednesday, then fire you on Thursday without so much as the blink of an eyelash. I was going to miss her. I wondered if anyone could take her place.

If you remember, my second firing by Leona involved Donald Trump. Leona had introduced me to Trump at one of Harry's birthday parties, in a year when they were on speaking terms (before the Empire State Building slugfest). "You should hire my genius," she advised. The Donald remembered Leona's advice. He hired Beber Silverstein to do the advertising work for a condominium in Palm Beach. Later he invited us to pitch his Atlantic City Casino. Several of us came up to visit the glitzy property and meet with The Donald back in his New York office, which was plastered with pictures of himself.

The morning of our scheduled meeting I was awakened by a 6:30 A.M. call to my hotel room from his agitated saleswoman.

"We need to meet for breakfast," she said.

"Sure," I agreed.

"Now. I'm in your lobby."

"Well, I'm not dressed. Give me fifteen minutes."

She was waiting for me in the dining room. "Did Donald pay for your ticket?" she asked.

"No."

"Did you ever have dinner alone with Donald?"

"No."

"Did Donald send you flowers?"

"No."

"Do you have a lunch date with Donald?"

"No."

She wiped her mouth delicately with the oversized hotel napkin, leaving an ugly lipstick stain on the white linen. "To tell you the truth, I'm just not comfortable with your shop. Donald said it was my decision, so I'm afraid this is it. Palm Beach too." She looked at me and smiled. "Sorry, but we can still be friends."

I got up and stood above the Donald's henchwoman, staring at long red fingernails pressed tightly into the tablecloth.

I said quietly, "Honey, I don't need any more friends. By the time I'm out that door I won't remember your name. But"—I raised my voice loud enough for Henry Kissinger, who was at the next table, to hear—"do me one last favor. Tell Donald he should have the guts of his friend Leona to fire people all by himself."

Rumor has it Donald has taken my advice.

Joyce Beber founded Beber Silverstein Group along with Elaine Silverstein in 1972.

FIRED FACT

Legendary directors get fired too. *Gone with the Wind* producer David O. Selznick fired director George Cukor, saying, "As a result of disagreements between us, we have mutually decided that the only solution is for a new director to be selected." Gossip at the time was that Clark Gable was upset by Cukor's homosexuality.[8]

FELICITY HUFFMAN ON
POPPING YOUR CHERRY

The first time I was fired was from a pilot with Ed Asner called *Thunder Alley*. Sometimes when you're acting, you think you suck and you don't, but this time I thought I sucked and I actually did! I remember I came back to New York and I got a call saying they were going to reshoot the pilot and I said a little wearily, "Oh, I have to go back to L.A." And then my agent added, "Without you." It stayed with me. I always think I might get fired during the first month or two of a new job.

The next time I was fired was from a Neil Simon play that was doing an out-of-town tryout before it was scheduled to move to New York. We did the read-through and then afterward the director said, "We're going to take the rest of the day off, and Felicity, I want to see you in the greenroom. Neil wants to fire you right now, but I think you can do it." Well, I made it through that out-of-town run, but I was in a panic the whole time, and then when the show came to New York, I read in the paper that I wasn't in it!

I've learned that everything is an audition. When they say it's a "work-through"—it's an audition. When they say it's a "read-through"—it's an audition. You always have to be on. But when I got fired that first time, Bill Macy, my husband, said to me, "Oh, you popped your cherry. Everyone gets fired." And it's true, you do feel like a show business veteran once you've been fired.

Felicity Huffman may worry about getting fired but has clearly made her mark with two Golden Globe acting nominations and her Emmy Award for Outstanding Actress in a Comedy Series for her work in *Desperate Housewives*.

DEAD MAN WORKING

Jason Kravits

It was a beautiful, sunny Monday morning when I got the call that I was going to die. This news, of course, came as a complete surprise to me, though looking back on it, I don't know why. I had been worried about how I was doing for several months. I hadn't been sleeping well. In fact, as I stood on the corner, looking at the caller ID on my cell phone, a feeling of dread washed over me. When you get the call from the man upstairs, chances are it won't be good news. I tried to be calm answering the phone. "Hello?" I said. I heard a deep breath followed by a loud exhale. "I have some bad news," the voice said. "Next week . . . Next week . . . you're going to die."

Okay, to be fair, he didn't say that exactly. What he said was "Next week your character, Richard Bay, is going to die," which, to any actor worth his ego, is the same thing. I had been working on David Kelley's *The Practice* for a full two seasons, first as a guest star, then as a recurring guest star, then as a full-fledged series regular. Things had been on an upswing. And now, quite suddenly, all of that was coming to an end.

David continued, "Listen, it's not your work."

"Right, sure, okay," I said, the whole time thinking, *It's my work.*

"I'm just not sure where else to go with the character, that's all."

I started to respond with, "Yeah, well, I've got a few ideas." But it came out more like, "Yeah, well, hey."

He went on after that, but to be honest, I didn't hear much. Not only was my mind going numb, but my cell phone was starting to lose reception. I walked back and forth on the sidewalk, pacing Wilshire Boulevard, contorting my body into all sorts of interesting positions, trying to get a good signal, but I could only comprehend the occasional phrase: "great two years (static) . . . different direction (static) . . . fishing cream." Fishing cream? I was just about to ask him to clarify when my phone, in some metaphorical gesture of empathy, went dead. I stood there for a moment, staring at my cell phone, trying to decide whether or not I should call him back—you know, so he could fire me more clearly. Luckily for me, I had just walked out of my therapist's office, so I was able to turn around and go right back in.

Now, for those of you who have never been killed off a television show, it feels like being dumped by your family, especially if your family pays you a lot of money on a regular basis. In Hollywood it's not that unusual. It happens every week on shows like *The Sopranos* or *Oz*. But if you're on those shows, you kind of have to expect it, don't you? You're in a prison or the mob. But this was *The Practice*, a drama about the legal system in Massachusetts, a state where they don't even have the death penalty.

Now I admit, I didn't take the news very well. I spent the next week wrestling with my fate, and when the day finally came that my death scene was going to be, well, shot, I was in complete mourning. I dressed all in black; I ate breakfast slowly, methodically, like it was my last meal. I paused to admire things I'd taken for granted—the early morning sunrise, the smell of the eucalyptus tree in the front yard. But as I drove down the 405, I began to feel somewhat complicit in my own demise. By the time I reached the exit for the studio, I was thinking to myself, "What are you doing? You know if you keep driving, you could be in Mexico by noon, and then what will they do? They can't kill you if you ain't there!" Then I remembered that it was television and they probably could, so I might as well collect my last paycheck. I took the exit.

Once I arrived on the lot, it became obvious that, if this was a sad occasion, a powerful day of mourning and loss, clearly I was the only one who was aware of it. To everyone else it was just a normal workday, except that every once in a while someone would see me and yell, "Dead man walking!" and laugh and laugh. I would pretend to laugh too and scurry back into my dressing room, turn out all the lights, and crank up the Radiohead.

Eventually it was time for "the shot," no pun intended because, yes, I was actually going to be shot—sitting in a car in a parking garage, riddled with bullets, slumped over the steering wheel, dead. Now, I had never played a death scene on camera before, and certainly not one of this magnitude. I was getting kind of nervous. We were about ten minutes away from rolling the cameras when I found the director. He's an older Frenchman named Jeannot whom I've worked with several times before. He's very good. If anyone could help me make this a powerful, meaningful, extraordinary exit, it was he.

"How do you want me to play this?" I asked. I waited for the wise words, the subtle guidance that would lead me through this tragic event. "Okay," he says. "You get in de car, you put on de seat belt, you hear *bang-bang-bang-bang-bang*, you do your Sonny Corleone in de tollbooth imitation, and you die. Facing de camera." Thanks, Jeannot.

No sooner was I in the driver's seat than Chuck, the special effects guy, who I swear to God was missing half a thumb, started excitedly waving his nine and a half fingers around the car. This was the guy in charge of my safety!

"Now, B car, that's the killer's car, will pull up just behind you, there. That's when you'll hear the caps go off. About fifty rounds. *Ratatatat.* At that point the pods will start to go off, blowing out about thirty holes on the side and back of the car. One's set right behind your headrest, so it'll look like you get shot in the back of the head, like Lincoln. Then the tires will blow out, this one, then this one, then that one. *Boom, boom, boom!*"

I was suddenly distracted by something straight ahead of me: a young blond man climbing a ladder tucked just behind a concrete pillar and pointing a rifle at me.

"Um, Chuck, who's he?"

"Oh yeah. He'll be shooting glass pellets at you. They explode on contact. But don't worry, we installed a layer of three-quarter-inch plexi between you and the windshield."

Three-quarter-inch? I thought. Why not a whole inch? "I think I'd feel better with one whole inch of plexi."

Chuck must have seen my growing panic, because he leaned into the car and said, "Don't worry, bro, I've done this for a long time. As long as you're sitting in this seat, you're completely and totally safe." Then he stood up and yelled *"Okay, everybody clear!"* Instantly people started scurrying all over the place, ducking behind concrete pillars, disappearing into the shadows. Chuck gave me a thumbs-up with his good hand, slammed the car door, and disappeared.

By the time they rolled the cameras, there was no one in sight. Not a cameraman, not a grip, not a best boy. All I could see were lights, cameras, concrete, and the barrel of a pellet gun. It was ominously quiet. I took a moment to collect myself. This is it, I thought: the moment between life and death, between employment and . . . un. I looked around at the emptiness. I placed my hand on the seat belt. I took a deep breath and as I let it out, I heard the screech of tires behind me. It was the B car.

Here we go, I thought. Dead man working.

Jason Kravits is an actor, writer, and composer. He played an assistant district attorney on *The Practice* for two seasons before his termination, literally.

FIRED FACT

You do the math: In 2005 unemployment rates were the lowest they have been since 2001. But who's making the money? Only the top 5 percent of the working public has seen wages rise. For the rest— 95 percent of workers—wages have remained flat or fell.[9]

THE DO-BEE

Martha McCully

If you could see me right now, the executive editor of *InStyle* magazine, sitting in my corner office in the Time-Life Building, you wouldn't think I am the type of person to get fired. Neither did I. I am a "Do-Bee." I do what's right. You remember the Do-Bees and Don't-Bees. As a Girl Scout I sold more cookies than anyone else in the state of Massachusetts. In high school I always showed up for class, handed in papers early, got A's, and went to Princeton. I was the president of Overachievers Anonymous. The one time I got a B+ in English my mother told me the teacher was jealous of me. And once I started working, the Do-Bee routine was pretty easy. I do like to work, I do like to be productive. I do a good job. So why was it that I had four jobs in four weeks one summer? Or lost a perfectly good job folding sweaters at the Lodge during college? Or, twenty years later, was asked to leave a big editorial job at a prestigious magazine?

Why? Because no one is safe from the F word. Even a Do-Bee gets fired and so did I. Repeatedly.

My string of firings began in 1980, during the summer I spent on Nantucket. Or should I say the four weeks I spent on Nantucket. Back then, going to Nantucket was the cool, preppy thing to do. So what if most of the Princeton kids had their wealthy parents rent them vacation homes on the water? I found a way to get there too. A friend and I leased a basement apartment somewhere in the middle of the island from a Frenchman who didn't speak any English. My first job was, what else, waitressing. I worked the breakfast shift. At 6 A.M. I would leave my dingy basement apartment and hitchhike into town. The Frenchman, who by the way had no fingers, would follow me every day in his truck and offer me a ride. I wanted to say, "Hey, just pick me up at home and stop this stupid charade," but I didn't. Besides, he couldn't understand English anyway.

At the restaurant I was on the lowest rung of the lowest ladder. When it was sunny, my station was inside. When it rained, I worked the deck. One day I made sixty-five cents. Total. I got annoyed and complained. I was axed on the spot. Swiftly, painlessly, like a kosher chicken.

My next job was at a silver jewelry shop on the same pier. It was the perfect job for me; after all, I had started a jewelry business in high school, complete with cards that read "Silver by Martha." It was pretty much all fun until the owner told me that I had to either sleep with him or leave. Again, I was a Do-Bee or, in this case, a Don't-Do-It-Bee. Ever notice that sometimes when you're being fired, it's presented as a choice when really there is no choice? They offer an alternative that you wouldn't dream of doing in a million years. The smarmy silver guy with the oily neck was that nonchoice for me.

Back in the restaurant business, I landed a coveted job in the kitchen at Obadiah's, a fancy Nantucket restaurant. My second day I forgot to close the walk-in refrigerator door, killing sixty or seventy innocent and really expensive lobsters. During this firing, a guy in a red bandanna really yelled at me, which I don't like when I'm being fired. No need for yelling. Do-Bees don't like to be yelled at. It makes us feel like we did something wrong.

Burning through a job a week, I went for the work/live combo and signed up to be an au pair, which I now admit was stupid. Growing up, I never babysat; I didn't even like to play with dolls. On the third or fourth day the perfect blond seven-year-old girl said to me, "You'd be really pretty if you lost thirty pounds." I immediately put down the Dungeons and Dragons and left, went to the pay phone, and called my mother in tears. Walking out on the kids, though I still believe it was for a very good reason, got me fired again. (Incidentally, I probably needed to lose twenty pounds, definitely not thirty.)

All of these little firings could easily be explained away by a Do-Bee. I believed I had done the right thing in each case. I now realize all of these incidents were just preparing me for the Big One.

If you work as a magazine editor in New York, you feel like you're about to get fired every day. Maybe you're not cool enough, if, say, you still carry a pre–Tom Ford Gucci bag or wear shoes with your Peds showing, or you show up puffy after the holidays, or in meetings you reference the Discovery Channel instead of E! But you can also be fired if you're too cool, if you get your name on Page Six more often than your boss does, or you get invited to the after after parties when she doesn't, or God forbid, you have a better seat at a fashion show, which I never did. Being the Do-Bee that I am, I was careful to never let those things occur, so neither of those firings happened to me. I was more in the "It's just time for a change" category.

At this point, seventeen years into my career, I had fired plenty of people myself, so I knew the lines, the looks, the euphemisms, the wording. Why does "letting go" sound like such a gentle, spiritually rewarding loosening of the tether? In fact it's a harsh, one-sided decision that will force you to stand in an unemployment line for a $226 check. Or why does "This just isn't working out" sound like you just can't finish the cross-word together and not like you are being asked to pack up and leave that very day, without saying good-bye to the receptionist who bakes you cookies or the creepy English art director you have a crush on or your drinks pal who is out sick.

I can remember the pink turtleneck and striped pants I was wearing that day, the ides of March, when my ex-friend, my boss, called me into her office. She couldn't look at me, and she was mumbling about what "we" would say. As she looked down at a fake manuscript, I became fixated on the back of her head and wondered if she was wearing a hairpiece. She had tried so hard to create a paper trail that I almost felt sorry for her. But not really. Inside I was screaming, "Wow, you're really firing me! This is kind of incredible! How much money will I get?"

When I walked out of her office, my own scalp was tingling and I felt kind of sick to my stomach. I thought about all the times the Do-Bee had done the right thing. Now I didn't have to anymore. I didn't have to care about the production meeting or the headlines and deadlines or about this season's bag. What a relief.

It made me feel a little bit better that other people at my magazine were getting the ax too, but they were given champagne parties and Prada bags as going-away gifts. I had to keep my firing a secret. (Only a true Do-Bee would agree to that kind of subordination.) I can't even tell you the name of the magazine because they made me sign an agreement in blood.

One of the worst things about being fired is that everyone who knows you is even more embarrassed. They don't know what to do, send flowers? Take your side? It's suddenly dangerous to be your friend. I was scratched off the invitation list of more than a few parties, events, and one wedding, because no one wanted to see me in the same room with my former boss. If they had only thought about the entertainment value!

One of the best things about being fired is coming to the

realization that it's not the end of the world, there is life after work, and that once the fear of firing is gone, you can actually make better choices. I'm not the Do-Bee I once was; I've been liberated. I know I'm still okay if my hair isn't blown straight every day or if my boots are from two seasons ago. Better yet, I'm no longer above shoplifting a few packs of gum here and there.

I do what I feel is right, not what someone else tells me is right. And you know what? I'll never worry about getting fired again. Let them fire away. I just hope it's at the beginning of summer.

Martha McCully is the executive editor of *InStyle* magazine.

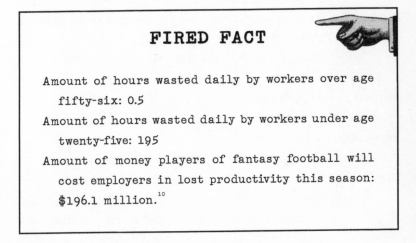

FIRED FACT

Amount of hours wasted daily by workers over age fifty-six: 0.5

Amount of hours wasted daily by workers under age twenty-five: 195

Amount of money players of fantasy football will cost employers in lost productivity this season: $196.1 million.[10]

DAVID CROSS MIGHT
JUST BE TOO BIG

At some point my friends were telling me stories that other friends had already told me. I was having a drink with Andy Borowitz when he said, "You know who has a great story? David Cross. You should call him." I said, "That's funny, I just talked to him yesterday."

Annabelle: David, as a child, what sort of employment did you feel yourself suited for?

David: Snake-handling rabbi. Following in the footsteps of the great Rabbi Lamar Shoenstein of Pensacola, Florida, who modernized snake-handling rabbiing by bringing it into the nineteenth century.

Annabelle: How close do you feel you've come to achieving this goal?

David: Not one bit. I have succeeded in the area of humorous craft services.

Annabelle: What's your best trait as an employee?

David: I can fart the alphabet.

Annabelle: Worst trait?

David: I'm a virulent sexist homophobic racist.

Annabelle: Do you remember your first job?

David: My first job was working as a busboy at Provino's in Atlanta. I believe what qualified me for this work was that my hands worked. Despite my rampant theft I didn't get fired. I was fourteen. It was illegal to hire someone that young, so they couldn't fire me. I stole five-gallon cans of clams and glassware. I love clams and what you don't eat you use as Spackle. I also painted houses, worked as a telemarketer. I sold all kinds of things. Once I was hired to raise money for Paul Simon's bid for the presidency and of course that didn't work out too well. I always got fired from those jobs. I did well at the audition but was bad at the job.

But my worst firing was when I worked at a law firm and was fired from the mail room with no notice. I can't remember what they said exactly, but my parting words were "Wait, I haven't had time yet to shit on your desk!" The best part of the story is I sued them for back pay. With the help of one of the attorneys at that firm, whom I became friends with, I gave a deposition and they paid me two thousand dollars. It was the most money I'd ever been paid until then. It was very satisfying.

If I did have to be fired again, there is one thing they could say that would soften the blow: "I'm sorry, your cock is just too big for this job. This is a little awkward, but we need someone with a much smaller cock for this job."

David Cross is not a rabbi but is starring in the Emmy Award–winning series *Arrested Development* and was the cocreator of *Mr. Show* on HBO.

MAUVE

Jack Merrill

After I graduated from one of the most expensive private universities in the country, I signed up with a temp agency. This agency specialized in placing "creative types," which meant you didn't have to have many office skills, just show up on time and look attractive.

They sent me to a variety of offices. I was receptionist at a law firm on the seventy-fourth floor of the Empire State Building. I worked at a brokerage house, a real estate office, and then—the big opportunity—Estée Lauder, the cosmetic giant, way up high in the General Motors Building on Fifth Avenue. I had a vague idea that they produced moisturizer or something. They needed me to work on a creative project that could take two to three weeks.

My job was to assist a creative team in making sure that cosmetic counters from Tokyo to Grozny had the proper displays for the Estée Lauder fall colors. Now this may sound easy, but it wasn't. There were all these languages to deal with and pamphlets explaining how to set up the counter displays correctly, the counter displays themselves, little colored leaves to strew about the countertop, the incentives to the salespeople to help them sell, and the special packages we were offering to convince the customers to buy. I thought it was fascinating. We were heading up a global operation! We were to have global impact! Women around the world were about to understand the new importance of mauve.

I pictured some poor blond village girl in Chechnya who had slogged her way down dirty unpaved streets to arrive finally in Grozny. I pictured her fighting off poorly dressed peasants, enduring the lascivious advances of big-city store managers, somehow surpassing other pretty blond Chechen village up-starts, and clawing her way to get to a coveted job at an Estée Lauder counter. That very same Chechen striver would be opening the box I had put together for her. She would be thrilled by the way I smartly organized everything inside. Opening the display card on her department store's no doubt dingy gray linoleum counter, considering which way it could be best viewed by the hordes of color-starved Eastern Europeans who were desperate to know what color to paint themselves. My happy Chechen upstart would daintily strew the little orange spray-painted leaves on her counter, being careful not to let them fall on the floor. She might even put some leaves in the display case itself, as suggested in her guide, handily written in Chechen. Then she would open the colors themselves, ten-tatively applying the makeup in the testers before introducing them to those desperate Chechen masses. We were spreading peace, commerce, and mauve.

I was beside myself. What an amazing place to work! Ques-tions started pouring out of me. Who came up with these col-ors? How many times a year did they change them? How long would mauve last? Is Estée still alive? How long had my fellow workers been involved in color campaigns? What was the last one? What would be the next? My creative team looked at me with a skeptical eye. Why did I care? Wasn't I somewhat overqualified for this job? How did I end up here in the first place?

If my creative teammates were becoming cold and distant, I wasn't going to let that stand in my way. Think of my Chechen striver! I was going to love spreading color around the globe—even if it was mauve. On my lunch break I scoped out the office. What a view! The windows look right into the roofline of the

Sherry Netherland Hotel. All angles and gargoyles, copper and gothic, with the green emerald of Central Park stretched out beyond. *I loved it!*

I think I was literally talking to myself, about how amazing it all was, when I noticed some female executives in an all-glass conference room nearby. They were all looking in my direction. One of them had gotten up to close the glass door. They were all so attractive and smartly dressed, busy no doubt with weighty issues concerning future territories and colors. This place was right out of a movie. I left them to their work.

After lunch some new people came into the conference room where we were working. They were interested in how things were going and seemed to take a special interest in me. My creative team deferred to them and that made me think that they were important. They must be here to check out the new guy, I thought. I mean, I had asked all these smart, probing questions and they must have recognized that I was just the kind of person that would be perfect to join the team permanently and maybe even one day head up the global reach of Estée Lauder!

One of them asked why I worked for a temp company when I seemed so bright and interested in everything from the fall colors to the layout of the office. Wow, I thought, someone as important as the Estée Lauder Corporation appreciated my innate understanding of global politics, style, and color. Then security showed up. Fully uniformed, they wore badges and actually carried guns.

I was told I would be paid for the entire week but that these nice fellows were here to escort me out of the building. Now. But first they were to look through my backpack, *and* they were going to frisk me.

I was so surprised, I just let it happen. The next thing I knew, I was in the General Motors Building's white marble lobby.

What had happened? I went from the global temp of the century to literally being thrown out, in like two minutes.

During the interrogation it all became clear. They thought I was some kind of spy. They thought I had infiltrated the important world of fall colors in the hope of selling the information to other companies who could piggyback their fall color lines and campaigns on Estée Lauder's. They were looking for microfilm, tape recorders, and documents that I had stolen. Maybe even the fall colors themselves. I was mistaken for a spy in the high-stakes world of corporate espionage. Maybe there was a future in the world for me after all.

After leaving the enigmatic temp world behind, Jack Merrill went on to be a founding member and artistic director of the renowned theater company Naked Angels in New York City. Jack performs stand-up on both coasts.

FRIED

Hillary Carlip

Mr. Billy Kent
Gazarri's Nightclub
Sunset Strip

September 17, 1973

Dear Mr. Kent:

Hillary Carlip here. You know, the performer you fired last night for no good reason? Sure, sure, you said it was because I put the audience, the entire club, and myself in danger, but that wasn't the case. I had everything under control and besides, I know you really couldn't care less if I was in danger. You haven't said a kind word to me since I started performing at Gazarri's every Wednesday and Thursday night three months ago.

I have a sneaking suspicion I was really fired for several other reasons.

1. You're an ageist. *When you hired me, you said that it wasn't a problem that I was just sixteen years old because if a situation arose, you'd just claim I never told you my age. But did you have to keep calling me "kid"? Come on, I've been making a living performing since I was fourteen and menstruating since I was thirteen. I'm hardly a kid.*

2. You're a sexist. *I've heard all about your "conquests" with the dancers and waitresses. Also, you've said to me on more than one occasion, and quite rudely, I might add, "You're the only female who does what you do. Shouldn't that tell you something?"*

3. You're a racist. *Well, not directly to me, but to Lavonne—the*

one black waitress at the club—and since we sisters stick together, you offended me too, saying your granddaddy owned a plantation.

4. You're a liar. *You said you'd pay me overtime if I did more than five shows a night. You owe me an additional $37.50 for overtime, but last night, when you fired me, you said, "We never discussed overtime." You lied right to my face, thinking you were so powerful and superior. Little did you know you had a piece of spinach caught in your front teeth and you looked like a motherfucking hobo!*

Now, regarding the "incident" last night. No one in the audience was in harm's way, nor was the club ever threatened. Okay, I may have been in danger, but that's the risk that comes with my job. If fire eating were easy, everyone would be doing it.

What happened was actually your *fault, or the fault of one of your employees, but since you're the manager, you have to assume responsibility for them anyway. So if you don't pay me everything you owe me—$25 for last night and $37.50 due from overtime—I will take you to court and demand that you also pay my doctor's bill of $46 resulting from last night's injury. That's right.* You're *responsible.*

Look, I've been eating fire for over a year now, and I have never had a problem. *I've been performing my act at your club for three months now and* I have never had a problem—*not when I've eaten fire torches or when I've swigged kerosene and blown it out at a flaming torch creating the crowd-pleasing ball of fire. But last night, for some reason unbeknownst to me, you or one of your employees turned on the ceiling fan without telling me, causing the fireball that I blew toward the audience to be blown right back into my face.*

Sure, some audience members freaked when they saw my chin on fire. But after I patted out the flames, I think I improvised a pretty clever comeback line, saying, "For your pleasure, I just made an ash of myself." I received the biggest applause I've ever gotten. Hell, most of the audience thought it was all part of the act and that I did it on pur-

pose! Well, until they saw me after the show and glimpsed the charred flesh on my chin.

Anyway, considering that the incident was caused by you or one of your employees and that no one was harmed except for me and my singed chin and *that the audience got a bang for their buck, I really don't see why you fired me!*

Well, maybe it had something to do with me standing up for Lavonne before the show and calling you a redneck honky. For that I am sorry, okay, I didn't know you were within earshot.

If I don't receive the $62.50 you owe me by the end of the week, you can expect to hear from my lawyer. That's right. Now try callin' me "kid."

Hillary Carlip

P.S. I just realized that fried *is an anagram of* fired. *Odd how both of those happened to me in one night.*

Hillary has left her gas-guzzling days behind her and has since gone hybrid. She is the creator and editor of Fresh Yarn, the online salon for personal essays, and is the author of three books, including *Queen of the Oddballs and Other True Stories from a Life Unaccording to Plan*.

Subject: One of Them Stories
From: Tate Donovan
Date: August 7, 2004, 10:53 A.M., PST
To: Annabelle

Dear Annabelle,

Sorry to hear about the job. It's miserable to get replaced. When I was fired, the only comfort I found was in knowing that everyone has either been there or will be.

Have I ever told you my story? It's a classic. In the late 1980s I was fired from the movie version of *Torch Song Trilogy* starring Harvey Fierstein. I don't know that anyone remembers it now, but it was a huge hit of a play and it made Harvey Fierstein and drag queens in general the hippest people alive.

There are few people in this world more fun to work with than a big bunch of drag queens. Especially if you're straight. It's like being an icy cold double fudge Popsicle in a group of sugar addicts on a hot day.

One day I phoned the production office to get my call time and the producer got on the line. That was kind of odd.

"Listen, Tate." Long pause. "Are you sitting down?"

"Yes." I stayed standing.

"We've decided to replace you with Matthew Broderick. I'm sorry, it was great to work with you, and we'll all miss you."

I sort of stammered off the phone and sat down in a daze. What if I hadn't called? How would they have let me know? The next morning real, real early, like 6:30 A.M., the phone rings. It's Harvey. You know it's Harvey because he sounds like Tom Waits meets Doris Day. He doesn't say hello, he just croaks, "Now you got one of them stories."

I was still asleep. "One of them stories?"

"Yeah, you know, how Hollywood fucked you over."

Great, I thought, just what I always wanted, but by the end of the conversation, I have to admit, he had made me feel much better. Apparently they had been trying to get Matthew all along because he'd done the play and he was family. That they'd miss me and all that crappy stuff that makes you feel like your life and career aren't really over. The effect of his kind words lasted almost as long as the phone call.

Amazingly enough, the worst of it was yet to come.

I dragged myself back to my New York City pad only to find that the majority of the film was being shot right in front of my building. The craft service table was stationed *right in front of my door*, and through my open window I could hear Harvey and the rest of the cast laughing and enjoying themselves like one big family. I couldn't leave my apartment for fear of running into everybody, and when I finally did have to emerge to replenish my dwindling food supply, I put on hats, slipping in and out when no one was looking, trying to avoid eye contact so that no one would recognize me.

In perhaps one of the darkest and pettiest moments of my life, I called the police to complain about the noise from the production. I thought all my prayers were answered when I heard the sirens blaring, only to peer down and see Matthew signing autographs and taking pictures with New York's finest! I'll never forget being in my little studio apartment, watching the arc lights streaming through the night air, as they filmed my character's big death scene in the park across the street. In between takes I could hear Matthew cracking up the crew. The assistant director was shouting "Action!" and "Cut!" above the grunts of Screen Actors Guild background toughs gay-bashing their way into film history. "Fag!" "Homo!" they screamed as they kicked him in the park, and I lay in bed wishing it was me being called "fag" and "homo." Finally the sun rose and I could hear a smattering of applause as the director cried out, "It's a wrap." I fell into a tortured sleep, certain they had missed me after all.

Tate Donovan has acted in more than twenty films including *Love Potion No. 9* and *Good Night, and Good Luck.* He currently directs and appears in episodes of *The O.C.* on Fox.

FIRED FACT

Thank you for firing me!

"I've been fired three times as a producer, once by David Letterman, once by Wayne Brady, but the first is my favorite. I was fired by Roger Ailes and I'm very proud of that. I think being fired by Nixon's media advisor really gives me credibility as a liberal."

Robert Morton, executive producer, *Weekends at the DL* and *Mind of Mencia,* both on Comedy Central.

Subject: Steak Today
From: Wildman Weiner
Date: May 5, 2005, 8:20 A.M., PST
To: firedbyannabellegurwitch.com

I've been fired more times than a postal employee's gun. And speaking of crime, I was hired by a prison to teach advertising design to a classroom of mugs, thugs, rapists, and robbers—even though most of the mugs, thugs, rapists, and robbers couldn't write their own names.

"Don't worry about it," said the warden. "It pays twenty-two an hour and you get a free steak lunch. Just teach them graphic design on the computers."

"But Warden," I said, "there are no computers. The inmates are just sitting and waiting."

"That's what inmates do," he laughed, slapping me on the back. "And don't forget," he added, "steak today!"

For the first month we had no computers, but I had a lot of steak. We sat in an empty room, me and men with names like Big Taco, Little Rambo, and Crazy Dogg, men who, in case they might forget who they were, had their names tattooed all over their bodies. Finally the computers arrived, but there was no software for designing graphics. "Don't worry about it," said the warden. "See you at lunch. Steak today!"

By the end of the second month, I had not taught these guys one single aspect of advertising design and no one gave a rat's ass. One day, when the inmates were having a philosophical discussion about the best way to break out of prison, I realized the computers came bundled with Microsoft Word. "All right, you mugs," I said, "we can at least write! Give me one hundred words on why you shouldn't be in jail!" "That's what I told the judge!" cried Dirty Weasel as I watched my students hunt and peck on their keyboards. Man, I felt proud, like I was making a difference!

That afternoon I got called over to the warden's table during lunch. "What's this?" he said, his mouth full of steak, holding a fistful of my students' writing.

"Essays in self-esteem, sir," I said. "Morale boosting."

"Self-esteem? What the hell for?"

"Warden," I said, "I'm trying to get the men to believe in themselves so they don't have to keep coming back here. I'm trying to rehabilitate them."

The boss man drew closer and looked me in the eye. "Mister," he said, "we don't want them rehabilitated. We want them just where they are because that's where our jobs are. Now pass me the A.1.!"

I didn't have any steak that day. I'd lost my appetite. But by the end of the day what I did have was my walking papers. "I like you," said the warden, "but if I let you stay on, we're gonna have us one helluva insurrection. Who the hell do you think you are, Robert Redford in *Brubaker*?"

As I was escorted off the grounds, my students emerged from the computer room, and I swear, Big Taco had tears in his eyes. And as we marched past, my head held high, I know I heard applause. Damn, I miss that grub.

Wildman Weiner is a Maytag repairman in Chatsworth, California.

I worked as one of three secretaries in a company that had a general manager, a sales manager, and a service manager. We three secretaries agreed that two of us would go to lunch from twelve to one and I would go from one to two. That way there would always be someone available to answer the phone and greet customers.

All three secretaries and all three managers could communicate with each other through an intercom telephone system. If one of the managers wanted to talk to any of the secretaries, he could press a button and it would buzz the secretary. Also, if a call came in and the secretary answered it, she could direct the call to the appropriate manager.

One day at about twelve thirty, halfway through the lunch hour of the other two secretaries, my buzzer rang. It was the general manager. I figured he needed something since his secretary was at lunch. I went to his office. His door was almost closed but not quite, so that when I knocked, it swung open. His secretary was sitting on the desk, with her skirt pulled up and her legs open. He was sitting at his desk, on his chair, with his head buried in her crotch. After picking up my mouth from the floor, I tried to get away without being seen, but he saw me. By the time I got to my desk, he was really buzzing me (I think one of them had pushed the buzzer accidentally before) to tell me, "Get your things together and get out. You are fired."

I will never forget that. It was December 22 and my birthday is the twenty-third. Also, the Christmas bonus was going to be given on the twenty-third. I had won about 60 percent of the silly performance contests they had, and that would have been reflected in my Christmas bonus as well.

Because this was a national organization, they had to fill out a termination form (with copies sent to the regional office, national office, etc.) and cite a reason for firing me. The reason was "substandard performance."

Needless to say, I could not use them as a reference when I went looking for another job.

P.S. Both the general manager and his secretary were married, but not to each other. She was an extremely religious person, always reading the Bible any chance she got.

FIRED FACT

Make money while firing folks!

PepsiCo follows other companies like Hewlett-Packard and Pfizer by initiating layoffs as it takes advantage of a huge tax break that was supposed to generate cash for new hiring. The American Jobs Creation Act, passed by Congress in 2004, is a tax break allowing American companies to bring foreign profits back to the United States at a discount of up to 85 percent off the normal tax rate. The result? Increased corporate profits but no new hiring. PepsiCo plans to layoff 250 employees by the end of 2005 and Hewlett-Packard will boot 14,500.[11] Send your thank-you notes to your congressman!

Subject: Dahling, It's Eva Gabor
From: Glenn Rosenblum
Date: May 7, 2005, 3:57 P.M., PST
To: firedbyannabellegurwitch.com

In the early 1980s I was the main receptionist for the Eva Gabor Wig Company in New York City. Besides being responsible for calling in wig orders to stores all over the country, the very first thing I was taught on the first day on the job was how to connect Miss Gabor from her home in Los Angeles to Merv Griffin through the 800 number. Although the Gabors came from some vague, unexplained Hungarian royalty, I loved the fact that Eva Gabor would call on the 800 line to save a dime. After all, this was *her* wig company, she *should* be able to call in and be connected to whomever she wanted. She'd call and say, "Dahling, how are you! Yes, dahling, connect me to Merv."

I was told to keep any conversation with her short and to the point. I was to put her on hold, dial Merv Griffin's private number, and announce her and then connect the lines. I had to resist the temptation to listen in. Seeing the two blinking lights on my switchboard made me wonder: Was she whining about *Green Acres* reruns? Was he whining about which hotels to buy and sell?

My chance to find out what they spoke about never came. I was let go. Something called a fax machine was being bought for the office and they were "downsizing." They no longer needed someone to call in orders since they could fax the wig orders. But who was going to connect Eva and Merv?

I always wondered. Did Eva ever speak to Merv again? Or did they fax each other their woes cross-country?

Glenn Rosenblum works for himself in Studio City, California.

Chapter 3

The Time You Deserved to Be Fired

Take this job and shove it, I ain't workin' here no more!

David Allen Coe

I have not failed, I've just found ten thousand ways that don't work.

Thomas Edison

I've been fired so many times, I sleep in a pink slip.

Taylor Negron, comedian

I don't want to work, I just want to bang on the drum all day.

Todd Rundgren

VIDEO, VIDEO

Paul F. Tompkins

In my lifetime I have been fired from two video stores. It's virtually impossible to get fired from *one* video store. Have you been to your local video store lately? The employees are far from helpful. So imagine what it takes to get fired from *two*.

The first one. Years ago, in Philadelphia, I worked at a video store called Beta Only. This store trafficked exclusively in Beta videotapes. This was in 1990! The same eight people came in and out of the store. These were people who could not let go of the dream of Beta. They liked to talk to us behind the counter about how superior Beta is to VHS. Apparently it has something to do with "lines of resolution." They would repeat this phrase over and over again, like it was a magical incantation. "You know, Beta has more lines of resolution." "Beta is so much better than VHS because it has so many more lines of resolution." Whatever lines of resolution were, they would somehow make even a terrible movie worth watching. "The movie *Partners* with Ryan O'Neal and John Hurt is a joy to watch with so many lines of resolution!"

Since the same eight people are not necessarily going to rent movies every night, there was a lot of downtime at Beta Only. I worked the evening shift with a guy named Jeff. Jeff and I would sit behind the counter for eight hours, making awkward conversation to fill up the crushing silence, as there was no TV in the store. Apparently the owners of Beta Only could not scare up a Betamax player to use in the Beta Only video store.

One night Jeff and I were both awful tired. We discussed this with each other in the absence of having anything else to talk about. I suggested to Jeff that we take naps. Jeff asked if we would nap in shifts. "Oh, no, Jeff, dear boy! I propose we take naps *concurrently*!"

So Jeff laid his little head down on the counter while I crawled *into* the counter and slid the door shut. It was pitch-black and womblike in there, like being in a sensory deprivation tank without getting all naked and wet. Our shift went by without interruption and we woke up at eleven o'clock, locked up our valuable product and empty register, and left.

After I'd worked there for about a month, I started to get more and more work doing stand-up comedy and so had to take more and more time off from Beta Only. Eventually the manager told me they were going to have to let me go because I was taking too much time off. I was fired but victorious!

All of a sudden it was 1994. I had just moved to Los Angeles and found myself absolutely destitute. I was so broke I couldn't believe it! I'd wake up every day and check my empty pockets: "This is impossible!" I had to get a job. It wasn't as easy as I thought it would be. I was turned down for the job of ticket taker at the Sunset Five movie theater after what *I* thought was a smashing interview. "Do you like movies?" "Yes." "Would you be able to stand at a podium a few yards from where a movie is playing?" "Absolutely." I did not get the job. I did not get the job of tearing small pieces of paper in half. So I moved a little further down the street and got myself a job at Tower Video in West Hollywood on the Sunset Strip. Back to retail.

The thing that happens in retail is that you start off chipper and friendly: "Hi! How are you? How can I help you? I like people!" Then eventually the bitterness sets in. "I hate you because you're not me!" I was miserable because I'd had a taste of making a living doing what I wanted to do, and then it was taken away from me. Here I was back behind a counter and I just couldn't make it fun anymore.

So I started stealing! I stole videotapes. I started small, tentatively taking one every week or so, but not getting caught made me cocky, and eventually I was taking two home every night. It was easy! And it was encouraged!

The unspoken understanding in retail is "They expect you to steal, that's why they pay you so little." There's an *arrangement*. I prided myself on the fact that I never stole money. I was no common thief! I was a gentleman bandit! I stole tapes for my friends. I was like Robin Hood! Kind of.

My girlfriend at the time expressed concern that I was liberating too many tapes and might get caught. We would practice the getting caught scenario so I could show her how simple it was going to be. She would say, "We know you've been stealing videotapes."

I would say, "I don't want to work for people who think I steal. I quit."

And that would be the end of it; they would get me out of the store and they wouldn't pursue it, because they *expected* me to steal. That's why they paid me so little. It was an *arrangement*.

One day I went into work, just like any other day. I wasn't sure what tapes I was going to steal that day, but what did it matter? I could steal movies I didn't even like, because they were free! I was getting dangerously close to the "lines of resolution" argument.

After about an hour I was called into the general manager's office. The GM was behind his desk and there was a security guy in the office with him. I was told to sit down. The manager said, "We know you've been stealing videotapes."

Instantaneously my plan completely crumbled. Could not make eye contact! Ears! Burning! Shame! All! Consuming! Because that's when I remembered that *stealing is wrong*. There's no *arrangement*! *Nobody* "expects" you to steal!

I was made not only to sign a confession, but to *write* one. "Dear Tower Corporation, I am heartily sorry for having offended thee . . ." Then the general manager told me to leave and added, "And don't come back here ever again."

Oh, really? I shouldn't come back? I thought. I shouldn't drop in a few days from now to see the old gang? "Hey, what's up, dudes? It's me, the guy who got fired for stealing! Anything good in new releases?" No?

That was almost ten years ago and it was my last day job. Sometimes I go to the Virgin Megastore to buy DVDs (coincidentally, right across from the movie theater that deemed me incapable of properly ripping paper in half). There's a guy who works in the DVD section who used to be the assistant manager at Tower. We are friendly and cordial when we see each other, but I can't enjoy the fact that I make my living doing what I love and he still works in a video store because we both know of my hideous, secret shame. That's not the way it was supposed to feel. It was supposed to feel victorious. I guess there really is no *arrangement* after all.

Comedian Paul F. Tompkins has not earned a living behind a counter since 1996.

SHORT ENDS

Jonathan Groff

An impressively tanned Rupert Everett was pitching his idea for a TV show to me, the writer NBC had decided should develop the series and write the pilot. "I'll play the British ambassador to the United States," he said in his plummy English accent, "and my assistant will be a dwarf. It will be quite funny, you see, because I'm very *tawwll*, and she's very *smawwll*."

I know I should have been grateful to Rupert for so elegantly explaining why we average-sized people feel the pleasure we feel when we see little people on screen, but instead I just had a sense of dread. "Here we go again," I thought. I have always had terrible luck with small things, including people. It's even resulted in my getting fired.

The first job I was ever sacked from was traffic reporter, and everything about the gig was tiny: the paycheck, of course; the converted maid's closet in the hotel which served as TrafficNet's home office and broadcast center; the goals of the organization—to provide rush hour traffic information for Providence, the capital of Rhode Island, "Little Rhody," the smallest state in the Union. And even the primary tool of the trade was minuscule: a 1982 Chevette. It was my job to report on the traffic via shortwave radio, while driving that Chevette (aka "Mobile 2") into the belly of the beast, the hellish interchange at the I-95 north-south split near I-195, where drivers would often have to slow down to *forty-five miles per hour* for several seconds as they merged into the traffic flow. Yes, Providence in June of 1983 was not yet the world capital—the Paris of New England—that it was to become. So even its traffic problem was small.

"Welcome aboard," said Dave Hemingway as he hired me. I certainly was a good candidate for the job. I had a clean driving record with a valid license. I had done the news at my college radio station and had a decent voice. I had good references: My friend Steve had driven for TrafficNet the summer before and had been a model employee. And I needed a job. So I returned Dave's warm handshake and made plans to meet him the next day at the hotel at 5 A.M. to pick up Mobile 2 and start my shift.

It was all set—until my alarm went off at 4:15 the next morning. In that instant I decided that I would never be a reporter for TrafficNet. I just couldn't bear the thought of waking up all summer long in the wee hours to drive a tiny car around an itty-bitty state with no traffic. I willed myself back to sleep, fully aware of the terrific "fuck you" I was saying to the man in the maid's closet whose only offense was offering me a job. I woke up at 10 A.M., feeling hungover with my own rudeness and irresponsibility. But I was too embarrassed to call Dave and apologize, and I didn't even know what I'd say. I really didn't want the job. So I avoided picking up the phone for two days as Dave left messages. I remember he wasn't so much angry as confused. Was I okay? Was there a misunderstanding? On the third day Dave's patience ran out. I was fired.

I can't absolutely prove that size was a factor in my next firing, which came years later. But I think it was. Jon Stewart let me go as a writer on his original MTV talk show, *The Jon Stewart Show*. As we all know, Jon is an incredible talent, but he tops out in the mid-five-foot range, max. I'm six two and, frankly, tower over him. I was easily the tallest writer on the staff. Now, I'll admit the possibility that my firing might have had something to do with the fact that I didn't pitch a single usable idea in my eight-week tenure on the show. Or it might not have. But how else to explain the fact that within a year I was hired by the six-foot-four Conan O'Brien and became his head writer nine months later?

I don't want to belabor the size thing about *The Jon Stewart Show* but there's more. In its infancy at MTV, the show had a fixation with little people (though that politically correct term was never employed in the writers' room). If there was a comedy problem, the solution was to "throw some midgets in there, have 'em run around, maybe one of 'em punches Jon." Midgets were big, to coin a phrase (and strippers too, for what it's worth). But try as I might, I never pitched a little-person bit that got on the show. In fairness, Jon had no choice but to can me.

My little-people issues continued to plague me even as I gained some career stability. One time at the Conan show I was in the hallway outside the studio just before showtime and took note of how many ridiculously costumed extras we had ordered up for the night's comedy piece, "Late-Night Characters Reenact the Seventh Game of the NBA Finals." There was Tomorry the Giant Ostrich. The enormous manatee. The Gaseous Wiener (a large, flatulent hot dog, naturally). All of them with basketball jerseys over their costumes, including former New York City mayor Ed Koch, who since leaving office had become a frequent walk-on character on the show. What I had forgotten was that segment producer Frank Smiley (five three, by the way) had arranged for a little-person actor to run out of the audience and pretend to fight with a guest who was appearing later in the show. The diminutive thespian had arrived and was standing behind me, but of course I hadn't seen him yet when I bumped into another writer, Chuck Sklar. "Boy, it's a real freak show here today," I said. Chuck glanced down to my right, then looked back at me. "They can hear, you know," he hissed. I could almost feel a pair of angry eyes boring into the small of my back.

That's nothing compared to what happened a year or so after that, just a few weeks before my first meeting with Rupert Everett. I saw a terrific HBO documentary about little people and their struggles and triumphs. One of the people chronicled was a guy I recognized from college. I didn't know him in school; in fact he had always seemed like a frat guy whom I wouldn't really care to know. But his life since college was inspiring. After enduring much skepticism from medical school admissions officers and directors of residency programs, he had become a star orthopedic surgeon at a top hospital, specializing in skeletal disorders that affect children, including dwarfism. He's married to an attractive woman and they have two children. I was thrilled to see how much he had done with his life and wished that I had actually known him in college.

I had the chance to amend that situation about a week later. I was walking up Sixth Avenue in Manhattan when I saw in front of me a group of three men, one of them a dwarf who from behind looked remarkably like my college classmate. Could it be him? I had noticed earlier that there were a lot of folks from a medical convention walking around my neighborhood with plastic IDs. Jeez, it *had* to be him.

So I walked quickly, got abreast of the group, and then slowly and deliberately looked over my left shoulder as I walked by. Bingo: same guy. But here's the stupid part. I never had a plan for what I would do if I confirmed it was he. So instead of saying anything, I just stared at him for an oddly long beat. He kept talking to his colleagues, but for a split second he met my gaze. I could sense a certain weariness in his eyes and in that moment I realized what I must have seemed like: another tall asshole stealing a gawk at a little guy.

I could have salvaged the situation with something like "Oh, hey, we've never met, but we know people in common from college and I saw you on TV and congratulations on the work you do, etc.," but that wouldn't have been in keeping with my pattern of terrible failure with regard to little people, so I decided to be content with what my stare had already communicated: "Hey, li'l freak!" I just turned and walked quickly uptown. It was one of the dumbest moments of my life.

So that's the collision course that little people and I were on when I sat opposite Rupert Everett and heard him describe his character, an underqualified ne'er-do-well playboy who ended up being Mr. Ambassador with a dwarf assistant. Of course it's not like the dwarf character was the only red flag. Rupert's whole idea was a bit flawed. He was quite convinced it was a classic "fish out of water" story. I suppose that if Mr. Ambassador were truly underqualified, it would technically make him a fish out of water. But in every other way, a British guy as the British ambassador would be a fish very much *in* water, which didn't seem all that entertaining. Here are some actual facts about the British diplomatic mission: the British embassy in Washington is actually British soil. Virtually every employee of the British embassy is British. The British ambassador primarily deals with British citizens and represents British political, diplomatic, and business interests, and if he's driving while doing it and happens to be on the grounds of the embassy, he's driving on the left. All in all, that makes for a very wet fish.

Three weeks later I had come up with my own take on the project. Rupert would play a rakish Englishman who had married a young Hillary Clinton–type American on a lark years ago and had even become a U.S. citizen. The marriage fell apart (though they never divorced) and he returned to England to a life of playboy irresponsibility. She went on to become a U.S. congresswoman. But she dies in office. With nothing else going on in his life, he accepts the governor's courtesy offer to finish out her term and then, against everybody's wishes, decides to run for reelection. That would be the beginning of the series. Rupert Everett in the U.S. Congress: an actual fish out of water. Like most TV sitcoms, it would probably suck, but at least it would be starting from an interesting place.

I flew out to Los Angeles to pitch to Rupert and his producing partner Marc. I felt confident as I drove to the meeting at Universal. And I felt even better when I got a call from Marc's assistant; Rupert and Marc were going to have some lunch during the meeting; would I care for anything? How incredibly thoughtful. I ordered a turkey sandwich. This was going to be a breeze. Over sandwiches Rupert and Marc would see just how much I'd improved their idea.

Rupert looked even tanner than at our first meeting, especially set against the white cotton fabric of the shabby chic couch in the Universal bungalow. As he and Marc began eating, I set to work on the pitch. My turkey sandwich sat untouched on the coffee table in a Styrofoam container. I realized it would be better for me to pitch first, then grab a few triumphant bites as they asked me questions about the finer points of the show.

Maybe, *maybe*, they laughed once. I don't remember. Mostly they chewed, as I spoke, faster and faster the worse it went. Finally I finished. Rupert looked at me affably. He may or may not have picked at his teeth with a tan bony forefinger as he thought for a moment, then said pleasantly, "It's quite a good idea, actually. But I'd rather do *my* idea."

And that was the end of the meeting. I actually give Rupert a lot of credit for not jumping across the room and stuffing my uneaten turkey sandwich down my throat while screaming, "Where's my dwarf, you wanker?" He couldn't have known my history, how I bungle any interaction with things of below-average size, how I was so completely spooked by his talking about a dwarf that I didn't include any mention of people of small stature in my pitch and had blown the job as a result. He just thought I was untalented, reckless even, for ignoring the gold mine which is the juxtaposition of tall and small. And he let me know all of that, politely, effortlessly, with a wave of his tawny hand.

Then it hit me. I had become Rupert's dwarf. He was a big movie star with a bad idea and I was a little television writer in his way. In dismissing me, he had illustrated the essential power dynamic of fire-er and fire-ee. He was very *tawwll* and I was very *smawwll*.

Which, by the way, is how being fired always makes you feel. Tiny. Insignificant. Adrift like a speck of dust. Even the familiar language of firing plays into this: "Your performance didn't measure up." "We are downsizing." "You can't write for midgets, get the fuck out."

I don't know how many of you have ever heard that last one, but I did, loud and clear. I slunk out of the bungalow, sweaty turkey sandwich in hand, feeling as small as the people and places I've either ignored or offended all these years.

Jonathan Groff was the head writer of *Late Night with Conan O'Brien* from 1995 to 2000. He currently lives in Los Angeles, where he is producing and developing television shows for NBC. His most recent effort was *Father of the Pride,* about a family of white lions who work for Siegfried and Roy. He was, in effect, fired by the 600-pound tiger who attacked Roy.

CRIMES AND MYTHDEMEANORS

Annabelle Gurwitch

I got the call as I was walking past Lincoln Center on a cold January evening. "Woody Allen loves you." It was the perfect New York moment. I could almost hear the sound of Gershwin playing behind me. I had always thought that working with Woody Allen was sort of the Good Housekeeping acting seal of approval. Now finally I was going to have my very own Woody Allen experience!

Earlier that day, at the audition for *Writer's Block*, one of two one-act plays which were to premiere off Broadway at the Atlantic Theatre, I was told not to shake hands or speak to Woody, which is the accepted protocol when in his presence. True to form, when I went to read for him, he had his hands over his eyes so you couldn't make eye contact. After I read, I was dismissed and called back in, and we spoke. He was very warm, funny, and supportive.

After I was offered the part, I started having fantasies. Late night tête-à-têtes with Woody at Elaine's. Rushing off for a nightcap with Woody and Mike Nichols. Brunching with Woody, Soon-Yi, and the kids in one of those big, rambling old New York apartments with the wraparound terrace overlooking Central Park. Together we would fire a bullet over off Broadway.

Sadly, there were even fantasies of a sexual nature. Although it is painfully obvious to moviegoers and Woodyphiles everywhere that I am a little beyond the age he prefers, this too was part of the fantasy.

Then I read the script. The play was a combination of *Hannah and Her Sisters*, *The Purple Rose of Cairo*, and an episode of

Three's Company. It just seemed so . . . so . . . "secondhand," as reviewers would later note. But I chose to put that out of my head because everyone had said he loved me and besides, no one says no to Woody Allen.

The first day of rehearsal was mostly spent trying to figure out if and when to say hello to him. His shyness is utterly intimidating. First of all, you can't believe how much like Woody Allen he is! All the throat clearings and little ticks, even the Woody wardrobe—down to the glasses, corduroys, sweaters, and laced-up Buster Brown oxfords. It was fun just to say his name, "Woody," before I asked a question, just because I could. Random weird thoughts would pass in and out of my head, like Hey, I could take his scribbled notes and sell them on eBay.

The atmosphere was very tense. Everyone wanted to be funny for Woody. One cast member was so obsequious to Woody, it was as though he were performing a colonoscopy with his tongue. In fact Woody seemed to really be making an effort to appear human, but he clearly hasn't spent much time developing his people skills. His rehearsal process was running the play over and over, with little to no feedback, a process I experienced as something akin to making a live organ donation.

Early on he asked to have private conferences with each cast member. I volunteered to go first. How was it? "About as much fun as the Nuremberg trial."[1] He gave me line readings for each of my lines right down to which words to emphasize. Now I understood why even the no-lipped, supergoyisha Kenneth Branagh sounded just like Woody in *Celebrity*.

There were so many things I wanted to know, but I was too afraid to ask—like, primarily, would he be writing more contemporary material? The jokes seemed to come from a drawer marked "things I wrote in the seventies." He was rewriting, though, and every day he would write new jokes for me and then he would tell me exactly how to say them.

I just couldn't believe the same person who had produced so many works of genius was producing something so, well, "disappointing," as critics would later note. But who am I to judge this American icon? I have hiccuped for five minutes straight while hopping on one leg on a sitcom, eaten a sandwich topless on HBO. I did an AT&T spot with Carrot Top. Yes, Carrot Top. Then again, I'm not a genius, so people expect less of me.

During the rehearsal process people would ask how it was going and I would always say, "Great! It's fantastic when the person you have idolized your whole life tells you you're terrible!" One day he said to me, "What you're doing is terrible, none of it good, all of it bad, don't ever do that again, even in another play." I was stunned. I believe I replied, "Well, don't hold back, Woody." Of course I am willing to entertain the possibility that I was terrible. In fact, I probably was.

I tried to soldier on, but when he told me, "You look retarded," I passed into a state of unconsciousness that I never recovered from. One morning I greeted another actor, who was experiencing a degree of panic himself, with "Hi, how are you?" "Being fired would be merciful," he said. I cheerfully replied, "Yes, I tried to get hit by a car on my way here today!"

I just couldn't believe that Woody Allen was ruining my Woody Allen experience! Luckily I didn't have to throw myself into traffic, because two weeks into rehearsals, I got an apologetic call from the director of the theater saying, "Woody needs to rethink the role." I was told he would write me a letter.

Woody's letter never arrived, so I have taken the liberty of composing the missive I would have liked to receive.

Dear Annabelle,

I am so sorry it didn't work out. Come and hear me play at the Pub next time you're in town.

Dear Annabelle,

When I said you looked "retarded," I meant it in that way that the disabled can elicit a warm fuzzy feeling and you just want to help them. And when I used the descriptive "terrible," well, sometimes terrible can be fascinating, like a fart that is so foul you can't stop smelling it. That is how I will remember you.

Or

Dear ——

I am sorry I never learned your name. I will put you in my next movie.

Yes, it occurred to me that in the two weeks we had worked together, he had only referred to me as "you" and by my character's name.

New York was his town and it always would be,[2] so I slunk back to L.A. like some kind of small-time crook.[3] Waiting for me at home was an anniversary present from a friend: a coffee-table pictorial of Woody Allen pictures! I thought maybe I'd try to get away from it all and go to Paris, but there was Woody doing advertisements to improve Franco-American relations! I turned the spines of his collected screenplays, essays, and videos around in my bookshelf to avoid his name and visage. Just seeing his face nauseated me, and I had to grab the remote control to change the channel every time I lighted on a Woody

Allen film on TV. I wanted to wallow in my depression but then I read that scientists had just renamed the depression gene the Woody Allen gene! I couldn't get away from him! For God's sake, I married someone who looks a lot like Woody Allen! It was hard to tell what was worse, the personal humiliation of being fired or facing the future in a Woodyless world with my Woodyesque husband. And just when I thought I was over it, I had a dream. In my dream Woody came to me and told me he had made a mistake and he put me back in the play. Then he took my hand in his crepey liver-spotted hand and then fired me again!

It sucks to be fired. My more spiritually oriented friends pointed out that "rejection is just protection and direction." Maybe, but that direction was downward, because this just sucked!

I was truly miserable and so I started asking people I admired if they had ever gotten fired and then I got really happy because I realized that I liked the stories about being fired more than the show I was fired from. Although I won't be appearing in the next Woody Allen project, at least I can say I had my very own Woody Allen experience.[4]

FIRED FACT

I felt like I was all alone but when I lost my job in April 2003 I was one of 161,000 New Yorkers separated from their jobs that month and one of 1,453,000 Americans who had been terminated from their employment that year.[5]

THAT GARLIN BOY

An Interview with Jeff Garlin

As I called around asking my friends if they had ever been fired, I happened to ring up the Garlin household. Marla, Jeff's wife, answered and said, "Oh, you have to talk to Jeff. No one's been fired more than Jeff, and he takes a lot of pride in his firings." I think it's true.

Annabelle: Jeff, as a child, what sort of employment did you think you'd be suited for?

Jeff: I wanted to be a comedian from the time I was eight. I was always getting into trouble. I was known around the neighborhood as "that Garlin boy."

Annabelle: That's never a good sign.

Jeff: No!

Annabelle: Did you work growing up and did your employers appreciate your sense of humor?

Jeff: I can't tell you how many times I've been fired. In high school I was fired from one end of the mall to the other.

Annabelle: Let's hear the rundown.

Jeff: Spec's Music.

Annabelle: How long was your tenure there?

Jeff: Not long.

Annabelle: How did it end?

Jeff: With the words "Take that hanger off your head, you idiot!"

Annabelle: Next?

Jeff: Fashion Conspiracy. I was knocking over mannequins. When they asked me who did it, I said, "It's a conspiracy." I was fired on the spot. My friend Eric was working there too, and they fired him with me. His mom cried when we told her, "I can understand you, but why him?"

Annabelle: Next.

Jeff: Salad Scene.

Annabelle: What were your duties there?

Jeff: Making salads.

Annabelle: How can you get fired for making salads?

Jeff: I was talking to friends while making salads.

Annabelle: Were you talking about salad?

Jeff: No!

Annabelle: Next?

Jeff: Plantation Movie Theatre usher. I kept pretending to interview the customers as they left the theater, asking if they liked the movie and trying get them to speak into my imaginary microphone.

Annabelle: What would you ask them?

Jeff: Well, we showed *Blue Lagoon* and I asked them if they thought there should be more nude shots of Brooke Shields.

Annabelle: What was the range of answers you got?

Jeff: "Yes" to "That's offensive."

Annabelle: After you were fired, did you go to see movies there?

Jeff: All the time.

Annabelle: Have you been fired as a stand-up?

Jeff: All the time. When I was first starting out, I was on the road a lot and they always put comedians up in a condo—read crappy apartment—and I was fooling around with another comedian and I threw a bowl of Fruity Pebbles at him and they stuck on the wall. Well, when I got to the club I was appearing at, I said to the owner, "Oh, by the way, I threw some Fruity Pebbles on the wall and I'll clean them up later." He said, "Get the fuck out of here. You're eighty-sixed." Well, I didn't know that eighty-sixed meant I was fired. I had to call my dad and ask him what it meant! Once, I was doing a gig in Ann Arbor, Michigan. I was watching the owner draw—he also was a cartoonist, and he had drawings of the comedians who appeared at the club up on the wall—and I asked when I'd get my picture up there. He said, "You don't have to worry about that, I'm firing you now."

Annabelle: Any more?

Jeff: Tahoe. I was following a magician who wore a cummerbund that spelled out "Tahoe" in letters that glowed in the dark. He got a standing ovation and I knew I was fucked. Now, I've bombed before, I've had people yell things at me. I've had people talking while I'm bombing, I was chased from the stage once by a guy with a giant dildo, but I'd never bombed to total silence before. Even the slot machines were quiet during my act. It was like all the power in Tahoe had gone out when his cummerbund lit up. It was an hour of pure silence. Afterward, the manager came backstage and fired me. He said, "Don't bother going back to your room, we've already packed your bags." They had my bags right there!

Annabelle: Do you worry about being fired?

Jeff: I should be fired from everything. I was just doing a gig that I thought if they fired me in the middle it'd be good. I asked them if they could name a swing state. About three hands went up. I was in Ohio!

Jeff Garlin stars in and is one of the executive producers of the award-winning series *Curb Your Enthusiasm* on HBO. He was recently fired as the host of *Fire Me, Please!* on CBS.

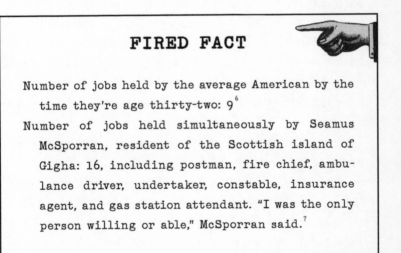

FIRED FACT

Number of jobs held by the average American by the time they're age thirty-two: 9[6]

Number of jobs held simultaneously by Seamus McSporran, resident of the Scottish island of Gigha: 16, including postman, fire chief, ambulance driver, undertaker, constable, insurance agent, and gas station attendant. "I was the only person willing or able," McSporran said.[7]

RIGHT ON!

Jill Soloway

Right on! Snap! Damn *straight*. When my agent called to tell me I was going to work on a black sitcom, I was thrilled. The executive producer of *The Steve Harvey Show* liked my spec script and wanted to meet me.

I quickly said, "Hell to the yes," *sure* she would love me. Finally I was going to be seen for what I was in my heart: a nappy-headed little black chile. For although it's probably clear from my name that I am a Jewess, it is perhaps less clear that I am no average white band. I was raised the only white girl in an all-black neighborhood, and hence I have always understood the phunky phat pheeling of my brethren Afro-Americans. How perfect that now I was going to be the only white girl on the staff.

I strode into my first day of work, confident the black people would love it when they found out just how down I was. I left conversational crumbs that let everyone know I could smell the difference between Dark & Lovely and SoftSheen, that I knew how to do double Dutch and what pork rinds tasted like.

I wanted the black people to know that, unlike most whiteys, I did not find it funny to see a man wearing a shower cap to the drugstore, because I understood that he was letting his Jheri curl chemicalize. I could sing all the words to "Car Wash" and "We Shall Overcome," and I understood the importance of keeping moisturizer handy at all times to battle ashy knees and elbows. I knew who yo' mama was, what "baby-mama" meant, and that your mama's friend's kids were also known as your cousins. And I knew how much I loved black guys for the way they *lovvvvved* women. All women. I was ready for the aggressive come-ons that would surely come my way.

But as my job unfolded, reality was slow to match my vision. I had forgotten that I was the one kind of woman that men—even black men—won't flirt with: pregnant. I wasn't "thick," as they called voluptuous girls, I was invisible. That was okay. I kept trying to get in anyway, tossing around the phrase "my baby's daddy" like it was the word "the." If they weren't going to appreciate my body, they might love me for how funny my inner black self was.

I jumped headfirst into the joke-pitching pool but quickly found myself getting blank stares. When I tried one of my favorite jokes—one that involved someone misspelling the word "birthday" on a card—someone asked, "Where's the punch line?" "Birfday" *was* the punch line, I mumbled as I sat my white ass down.

I decided to change strategies and pitch jokes that were funny to me. Sadly, though, no one there knew what a knish was. My super-Jewy stream-of-neuroses observational humor was met with "Who would ever think that?" or "No one really talks like that."

I tried to get the hang of their comedic stylings. Metaphors and similes seemed to be popular: "He jumped on that government check like Star Jones at a buffet table." "That dog tore into him like Whitney Houston on a chicken bone." And "His car note was as big as Esther Rolle after free Sunday brunch." I cracked the black joke code: black actress plus food equals hilarity.

When my baby was finally due, I had to leave the show, figuring I'd study up over the winter and be able to come back with some terrific new material about Patti LaBelle and corn bread.

But when the next season came around and it was time for me to go back, my agent called. He had talked to the show runner: I wasn't being asked back.

Not being asked back is the equivalent of being fired in Hollywood.

"Not being asked back?" I was appalled. "But I'm so funny, and down, and . . . black!"

"To be honest, she said she thinks you'd be better writing for a . . . white show."

"A white show? *Better on a white show?*" Now I was outraged. "What if someone said that a black writer would be better on a black show? I'm gonna call somebody, and say something!"

But after I couldn't think of anyone to call, and a few days passed, I realized she might have been right. Maybe my black references were a little dated. For all I knew, Dark & Lovely might not even be on the shelves anymore. Flipping around the TV channels, I could see that the characters on *Will and Grace* were spouting all sorts of Jewy hyperobservations—just like me! Maybe, just maybe, I could get a job there. The more I thought about it, the more I was sure the writers there would be able to see through this Jewish girl to what lurked behind: a big ol' gay man. Yes, in chaps and a handlebar mustache.

My agent got me an interview at *Will and Grace.* I spent the morning before my meeting downing Coca-Colas at DuPars in the nearby mall. Fast and funny, fast and funny, fast and funny, I thought. I must have been too fast and funny in the meeting because half the room looked at me as though I had spinning spirals for eyes. Or maybe I just wasn't gay enough.

My luck turned when I had an interview on *Six Feet Under.* Inappropriate jokes, my gay sensibilities, even my Jewish melancholy I'd had to hide as a sitcom writer—all were welcomed. I got the job and somehow managed to not get fired—or not

"not get asked back"—for four whole years. In fact, in my very first episode, there was a Jewish guy who died from masturbating while hanging himself from an exercise bar, a sexy girl rabbi who was highly inappropriate with Nate, and a whole sequence where Claire spent a week at a hippie-dippie rural retreat where people danced around naked and my friend Brett shimmied with her top off. Let's see, Jewish, sexy, some of my closest friends naked on national television—I guess my voice was finding an audience after all. Right on.

Jill Soloway was a writer and producer on *Six Feet Under*. She produces *Sit 'n Spin*, a monthly reading series in L.A., and is the author of the comedic memoir *Tiny Ladies in Shiny Pants*.

FIRED FACT

Fired former Tyco CEO Dennis Kozlowski, known for his lavish lifestyle and purchase of a $6,000 shower curtain and a $2 million birthday party for his wife, was convicted of stealing more than $600 million from Tyco and sentenced to up to twenty-five years in prison. His severance pay from Tyco originally topped $135 million; the amount was later reduced to $30 million. He'll need it because he was fined $70 million, and the shower curtain might just come in handy in prison.[8]

FRIENDLESS

Fisher Stevens

It was about nine years ago, now that I think about it. Six months earlier I had finished a run on Broadway in *Carousel* and then gone on to London to shoot a film called *Hackers*. But when I returned from London, everything seemed to come to a halt. I felt as cold as the unbearable temperatures outside. I started getting paranoid that I would never get work again. Finally my phone rang. It was my manager saying he had an "offer." An offer—music to my ears! I wouldn't have to go through another unbearable audition. The offer was a guest shot and possible recurring role on this "hot new sitcom that everybody loved."

"A sitcom!" I shouted, "I don't do sitcoms! I am an actor—a man of the theater!" I had purposely avoided sitcoms up to this point in my career and I'd never even heard of this "hot new show that everybody loved"!

"Hey, Fish, they'll fly you to sunny L.A. first-class, put you up in a fancy hotel, and pay you well—baby, what's wrong with that? Try it, you might like it. Besides, it will be good for you to show your face in L.A. I'll fax you your scenes."

The scenes weren't bad. A bit jokey, but much better than I expected. I would play a shrink. I had had lots of experiences with shrinks, and it would be nice to get out of the cold and visit my friends out west. What the hell, I might even like it. After all, it was only three days' work. I immediately dove into the script, figuring out who my character was, visiting my own shrink four times a week. What were my character's parents like? What did he eat for breakfast? Where did he go to college and then grad school? Did he see his patients on a couch or a chair? Being a slow study, I worked the text over and over in my head. I was actually starting to get excited about playing this character and experiencing this new world.

When I arrived at the studio, I felt a bit nervous. The stage was freezing cold. The cast, two of whom I'd met before, were very nice and welcoming. They all seemed so happy working together and were all attractive and the men had such thick hair. I immediately felt pale and like I needed a nose job. Next I was shuffled off to meet the writers and producers. They leapt up and thanked me for doing "their little show" and then handed me a new cranberry-colored script. "We had to make a few changes; it's much funnier."

My throat got dry. "A few changes." I hope not too many, I thought. I had memorized everything.

"We go on in two days."

I sat in the corner and read it over. I was flabbergasted. The only thing that had stayed the same was that I was still playing a shrink. "This was not the script I signed on to do. Can't we go back to the old script?"

"No, no, this is much funnier," said the producer. "You'll see it works. You'll hear it at the read-through."

We began. The minute I opened my mouth, these tremendous guffaws started coming from the writers across the room. *Ha, ha, ha!* I thought something was going on at another stage; I couldn't have been that funny, not with these stupid lines. They were laughing at everything. I thought the writers had Tourette's. "Mouth attached to nipples—I can't say that, it's not funny."

"It's hilarious, just say it."

I did not train as an actor for fifteen years to say "nipple," I thought. Ninety percent of my lines had changed for the worse.

At the dinner break I started complaining to David Schwimmer. He tried to comfort me and told me this is how sitcoms worked. They changed the scripts up until shooting. I told him he should get off this piece of shit and that it would kill his career and he would start developing bad habits as an actor. He just looked at me politely and sort of smiled. I could tell the whole cast was starting to think I was an asshole theater snob from New York. I made one final plea to the producers to go back to some of the old script. I compared the old one to a great novel or a beautiful meal and the new one to tabloid junk. The producer basically told me to shut up and say the lines. "The network loved the *new* script."

I couldn't sleep the night before the taping. I studied my new lines, trying not to judge. I wanted out of Hollywood. I would do an Ibsen play in some outdoor theater in Minneapolis.

Finally the hour came.

It all went by so fast, it was almost surreal. I do remember saying the "nipple" line and getting a huge laugh. Most of the cast ignored me. They were pros, so calm and relaxed, nothing seemed to rile them. I loosened up a bit but mostly I was just trying to remember the new lines. When it was over, the producers came up to me, gloating, "We told you it was funny." Then they practically shoved me out the door and said, "Thanks, check's in the mail."

When I said good-bye to the cast, I felt sorry for them that this was going to be what their lives would be like for the next year. I told them to look me up when they were in New York. "Maybe we can do a play?" They politely smiled and I could tell they couldn't wait to never see me again.

Back in New York things were still a bit slow, so I took the first play that came along—an off-off-Broadway show about a gay junkie in the East Village who was going to rid New York of stray dogs and cats. In retrospect, the writing was a lot worse than the sitcom but I didn't care. It was theater and I was an actor.

A few weeks later I was walking down the street and people started coming up to me, saying how funny I was on the show. Somebody even asked me if I was a real shrink.

When I had to do press for the film I had done in London, the journalists didn't even ask me about the film. All they wanted to know was what it was like to work on the sitcom. One of them even quoted the nipple line and started laughing hysterically.

Meanwhile the next winter was approaching and once again New York was freezing. My movie tanked but I kept getting recognized from that sitcom, so I thought what the hell, let bygones be bygones. Since everyone seemed to love me on the show, maybe they'd want me back after all. So I called my manager and asked him to see if they would write me back in the show. There was a long pause and then he burst out laughing. When he finally stopped laughing, reluctantly, he said he'd ask and call me back in ten minutes. I waited anxiously by the phone. When it rang, I grabbed for it. My manager said, "I talked to the producer and she told me, 'Over my dead body would Fisher Stevens ever appear again on any episode of *Friends.*'"

As an actor, Fisher Stevens has appeared in *Hackers, Early Edition, Short Circuit,* and *The Flamingo Kid.* He directed *Just a Kiss* and produced *Slow Burn; Yes, Piñero; Uptown Girls;* and *Swimfan.*

BILL MAHER:
WARM BODY TELLING JOKES

Back in 1980 I was hired to be a headliner for the first time. It was a very painful experience. I had only been doing comedy for a year, and some restaurant in Cleveland had called and booked me; they had a back room and some extra chairs, and they said, "Hey, let's do comedy." There was a lot of that back then. In fact the first job I ever did was at a Chinese restaurant in Paramus, New Jersey. Larry Miller and Eddie Murphy, who was still in high school, were on the bill. We each got twenty-five dollars for the night.

Anyway, headliner I was not. But comedy was just exploding, and so people were looking for warm bodies telling jokes. I didn't have an hour of material if I scoured my notebook. I had some jokes like the beginning of my "I'm half-Jewish, half-Catholic" routine that I did on *The Tonight Show* a couple of years later, but at this point, I was light-years from being able to headline. When I was young and bad, I was also bad in the sense that if it wasn't going well, I'd get hostile with the audience, so as the evening progressed, not only was I bombing, crummy at the job, and inadequate to the task, but I quickly alienated the audience. When you do that, you bomb even if you are funny. They won't laugh at you once you insult them and blame them for your inadequacy. You can tell the greatest jokes in the world and it won't matter. It was an ugly scene. I was supposed to do the next day, but the manager said, "No, you're out of here." We had an argument about whether I was going to get paid. I felt awful. The next day I just wanted to get out of that town. I ended up getting snowed in and I waited twelve hours at the Cleveland airport. I was afraid the whole time that someone would recognize me from the gig I had gotten canned from.

When I was twenty-nine, I was hired to do a talk show. I had just done a series called *Sara* with Geena Davis and Alfre Woodard, and by then I had done some *Tonight Show*s and so I had some heat on me, as agents and managers say, so King World and Motown (now there's an axis of evil if I ever heard one) called me in and they said, "You're the guy." I remember vividly in the meeting they said, "We want someone fresh and new. We don't want Robert Klein or David Brenner."

We worked for a few weeks writing sketches, some of which were pretty good, but they put me with Dinah Shore's producer, and I didn't have the clout to fight it. I didn't even know what a producer did. I figured his name was Fred and Johnny's producer's name was Fred—well, I guess you gotta have a guy named Fred. We never shot the show. We did a test shoot, one test shoot. We should have been doing a hundred test shows—that's what we did when we started *Politically Incorrect*—but you take a twenty-nine-year-old kid, and yeah, he's not that good.

After they canned me, I turned on the TV one night and there was Billy Preston, who I had rehearsed with as my bandleader, with none other than David Brenner. I just thought, "Oh, they kept the bandleader."

At some point one of the King brothers called me and I got paid off—$17,000. At the time I thought I beat them out of a small fortune; meanwhile they were making like a billion a year on *Wheel of Fortune*.

One of the main lessons people should learn in life is that you can never tell when something happens to you whether it's ultimately going to be good or bad. It may seem bad at the time and it's really good, or it may seem good and it's really bad. That's really true in showbiz. I was really upset when *Sara* was canceled. But I remember now that when the *TV Guide* came out announcing the show, under my picture it had said, "Bill Maher as the office creep." If that show had lasted, I'd have become the new Ted Baxter. Getting fired off *Graveshift, Night Shaft*—whatever that King World show was called—that probably was a good thing too. I don't think anybody twenty-nine years old is going to be good at hosting a talk show. Hosting a talk show is a man's job. Even when *Politically Incorrect* was canceled by ABC, I had been doing it for nine years, and I was tired of it but I wasn't going to walk away from it, so when I said the thing I did that ended the show, well, it really wasn't so terrible. I was ready to move on.

Bill Maher is the host of *Real Time with Bill Maher* on HBO.

FIRED FACT

As a testament to the power of late night comedy shows, Bill Maher's *Politically Incorrect* series-ending comments attracted the attention of the White House. At a press briefing on September 26, 2001, Ari Fleischer, press secretary to the president, said, "It's a terrible thing to say, and it's unfortunate. All Americans need to watch what they say, watch what they do. This is not a time for remarks like that; there never is."[9]

THE POSTMAN NEVER RINGS TWICE

Richard Colburn

I was seventeen years old, six months out of school. I wanted to be a professional snooker player so I took a job at my local post office in Perth, Scotland, to keep me in practice money. The job was only for two months over the Christmas period and it was on a casual basis. There was no uniform and they basically phoned you when they needed you.

I was a very willing and hard worker and the powers that be in Perth were suitably impressed, so they decided to keep me on. I was starting to really enjoy the job. The whole snooker thing was even taking a backseat to the security and the sense of community that the post office offered.

After six months the bosses pulled me into the office and told me if I kept a clean sheet until I was eighteen, they would take me on full-time. It was the news I wanted to hear and I was delighted. I was seventeen and a half by this point, and I had just passed my driving test, which was good because it meant you didn't have to deliver the mail on foot so often. That was a bonus because quite often you would end up delivering mail in a dodgy bit of town and then be confronted by several drunken undesirables looking for their unemployment benefit checks and any other checks for that matter. A post office van provided you with the means for a very quick getaway, necessary because these guys were thirsty and booze doesn't buy itself.

It was about a month until my eighteenth birthday, and I was looking forward to full-time employment within the ranks of the Perth post office. It was a Saturday and particularly busy, with lots of mail to be delivered. I had arranged to go to a football match that day, which meant I had to finish work at midday sharp. I decided to take my own car for quickness; my grandfather had given me the car as an early birthday present a few weeks before. I had two bags' worth of mail to deliver and several loose bundles of mail as well. As I was grappling the mailbags into my car, I put the loose bundles on the car roof. Then I headed off. I got to my first drop-off point, about half a mile from the office, and started to sort out what mail would be delivered first. I couldn't find the two loose bundles anywhere. I checked the mailbags over and over again but couldn't find the bundles. I had that horrible feeling you get when you lose your passport ten minutes before you're due at the airport to go on a dream holiday. It was then I remembered that I had put the bundles on my car roof when I was putting the mailbags in my car. I retraced my route for about an hour but couldn't find the bundles. I had a dilemma. If I admitted to losing the bundles, I would be in serious trouble, but if I didn't, there was a fair chance that somebody might pick them up and stick them back in a postbox and I would be found out. I decided I had to report the loss to the bosses. They were very understanding; in fact so understanding they sacked me. I couldn't believe it; I was only a month away from being made full-time. It seemed like a body blow at the time because the very thing I was trying to avoid, a full-time job, had seduced me.

You think you're going in one direction in your life, then something happens that takes you in a different direction, and you're back to square one. At the time I thought I'd been hard done by, but looking back, I see it's a case of one door closes and another one opens. If I hadn't been sacked, my life would've gone in a completely different direction, not necessarily bad, just different. After I was fired, I moved to Glasgow and lived in an apartment that happened to be next to some members of a band. One day their drummer didn't show up and they happened to hear me playing bongos next door and invited me to sit in with them. That's how I ended up in a band.

You don't know whom you're going to meet tomorrow. In fact you don't know whom you've already met who could change your life.

Richard Colburn is the drummer for the indie rock band Belle and Sebastian.

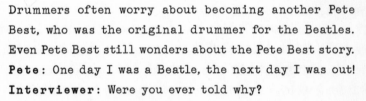

FIRED FACT

Drummers often worry about becoming another Pete Best, who was the original drummer for the Beatles. Even Pete Best still wonders about the Pete Best story.
Pete: One day I was a Beatle, the next day I was out!
Interviewer: Were you ever told why?
Pete: No, but let's look at the theories. I can't accept the drumming theory, as when we came back from Germany, other groups copied my style using the loud bass drum. As for Ringo being a better drummer, well, he was replaced on "Love Me Do" as well, wasn't he? The hairstyle? That's all rubbish; it was never even discussed. Personality? I took part in all the crazy stunts and drinking. A rumor around the Cavern was that it was because I turned down Brian Epstein's advances, but I don't believe that. At the end of the day two people still alive know the reason. We may all read about it in the newspapers next year or we may never know.[10]

BA-LOONEY TUNES

Matt Walsh

In the summer of 1990 in the town of Chicago, like five million other guys in America, I was trying to make my living as a stand-up comic. Most of the club owners in Chicago were fat, cheapskate, pickled alcoholics who didn't really warm to my postmodern comic stylings, so I found myself needing a job to subsidize my artistic journey. A stand-up friend had been working as a singing telegram artist and had said the job was awful but you worked out of your car and you could do it while you were high. Awesome, I thought.

In no time I was off to my interview/audition at the home of Seth and Gail in beautiful Evanston. Seth and Gail ran the business out of their home but it quickly became apparent that it was Gail who would pull the trigger on my hiring. Gail was a fortysomething mother of two who was completely humorless. She was, however, impressed with the fact that I was a performer and proceeded to tell me about the various writers, directors, and musicians who were currently in their employ. "Wow. You guys are just like the movie studios of the thirties and forties," I joked. Gail found nothing witty about my analogy. But clearly Gail could sense that I had tremendous talent, and soon the only formality left was for me to give her a sample of my awesome singing style, which consisted of producing one or two low-range notes then dropping down to an inaudible level to mouth the words for all the other notes. However, my philosophy on singing was that anyone could sing as long as they sold it. Hadn't Mark Knopfler been talking his way through albums for years? So I readied myself to belt out a version of the compulsory "Happy Birthday" (even though we could not use this tune on the job). Before I could wow Gail with my level of commitment, she halted me and took a seat across the room in a chair facing the wall. "I'm sorry but I can't look at people when they sing. It makes me nervous." Was I being incorporated into some weird fetish of Gail's? I didn't push for any backstory, instead I belted out the loudest, most-adrenaline fueled, indoor version of "Happy Birthday" anyone had ever sung. When it was over there was nothing but awkwardness for everyone involved. I had "plugged in" when the venue had called for acoustic. It was, however, effective. Within minutes Seth was laying out a stack of employment forms for Gail and me to go through. Once the paperwork was done, Seth took over and began a monstrous thirty-minute tutorial on how to tie a colored ribbon to a colored latex balloon. I granted him his attention to detail because their company was called Ba-Looney Tunes. Somewhere between Seth's over-explaining of the balloon knot and Gail's ignoring the visual aspects of song performance, I realized any moron with an insured vehicle would probably get hired.

Well, I was part moron on my father's side and I needed the money. After the balloon tutorial, Seth handed me the boxes and bags that contained balloons, ribbon, and the costumes that all Ba-Looney Tunes crooners needed, including: the purple gorilla, the cowboy, the pink elephant, Zorro the kissing bandit, Cupid (complete with suction cup arrows), and of course a clown. Seth finally rolled out an eighty-pound helium tank from the side of the garage and said, "Where do we put this?" It seemed I was also required to transport the completely safe, inert gas helium in my car. We managed to wedge the five-foot tank lengthwise between my two front seats, leaving the helium nozzle precariously balanced just beneath my gearshift.

My first dispatch came the next day from Gail. I was to go to

Park Ridge to sing to Sylvia on her eighty-eighth birthday. In-cluded in Gail's message was the number and color of balloons to inflate, and the character I would play: Cupid. Son of a bitch. The first one out of the gate and I gotta wear the formfitting costume of the love assassin.

The address turned out to be a nursing home three miles from O'Hare Airport. Being a good employee, I got there a half hour early to change into my pink tights and flesh-colored uni-tard. Already compromising the integrity of the character, I had decided there was no way I would wear the tutu that came with Cupid. After banging my knees on the steering column, I managed to get into character. I then inflated the balloons, tied perfect little knots to them, then filled out the card with the message from Sylvia's son, Jeremy. Armed with fifteen colored balloons, a plastic bow and arrow, and two loosely memorized tunes, I psyched myself up and left the comfort of my Toyota changing room.

I found Sylvia in the nursing home cafeteria with some thirty other residents. As I walked over to her in my pudgy, flesh-colored glory, she was just finishing up some crackers. A youngish man in a suit was seated next to her. Fearlessly I launched into my crowd work: "Sylvia, someone wants to wish you a happy birthday." With crowd work checked off, I swung into the first of my two event-appropriate songs. I went to the classic, "Oh someone is celebrating, oh who in the world could it be . . ." Halfway through my Ba-Looney Tune I noticed that Sylvia was full-on weeping. I felt awful. Had I scared her? Was I that bad? Then the man seated next to her said, "Mom, it's from me. I got you a singing telegram for your birthday." I thanked God for Jeremy and his crowd work. Jeremy instantly realized I was overwhelming his mother, so he cut me loose and took the balloon bouquet. During my walk of shame out of the cafeteria, no fewer than three residents asked me, "Who are you supposed to be?" The missing tutu was throwing them. As I changed back into my civvies in the parking lot, I vowed this was my last day of work.

The next four gigs were dismal: a purple gorilla at a biker gang picnic, a Superman anniversary at a plastics factory near the Wisconsin border, and a couple of awful renditions of a clown at kids' parties.

My relationship with Gail had also begun to slide. My general resentment of the job and the whisperings of dissatisfaction Gail was hearing from clients had begun to eat away at both of us. I began to dread Gail's calls, each one a short death sentence. What kind of ass would she force me to be this time? The upside of all this was that the job was pretty easy. I didn't have to go to an office, and I could get in and out of any gig in about five minutes.

It was about this time that I started bringing friends along to break the monotomy. The friends I brought along were always other comics, equally desperate for money.

The first friend I brought with me was Rick. Rick was crazy. The kind of crazy that would make him stare down guys at a party until they had to be held back from kicking his ass, the kind of crazy that made him strip naked in crowded rooms and walk slowly out the door, the kind of crazy that eventually made him drive his cab into the Chicago River. But Rick was without a doubt the funniest person I had ever met. Whenever I had a Ninja Turtle gig, I would bring Rick. He would create a fictional character by assembling various costume parts from my theatrical trunk: a purple gorilla head, a little Zorro cape, maybe a dash of clown shoes. It was always new and exciting. Once dressed, Rick would storm the kid's party and say, "My name is Kiefolver and I have come to ruin this birthday party."

Then I would show up as Donatello or Michelangelo or whichever Turtle they had requested—they were all the same hard plastic turtle shell and green coverall, just different colored bandanas—and I would shout, "I am here to save this party and defeat my mortal enemy." Then we would have a prolonged, sloppy fake fight. Lots of shoving and slapping each other with plastic swords. Oftentimes it would just break down into full-on wrestling. We would tumble on top of each other for way too long, all the while trying not to crack up. But often we couldn't help from laughing at our moronic high jinks. We would collapse on the floor breathless and in tears, silently laughing for large chunks of time while all the adults in the room looked on in bewilderment at the silently vibrating costumed characters on their living room floor. My firing was an inevitability.

My irresponsibility peaked at a birthday party for a boy named Kevin in Lake Forest. It was a Ninja Turtle gig and I had brought my friend Adam along. It was Adam's first Ninja birthday party. On the drive up to the gig, I gave Adam the Ninja protocol in Sethlike fashion. "You show up as my enemy, I show up as Donatello, we fight, I win, I send you to get the balloons, we sing 'Happy Birthday, dear Tony,' or whoever, and then we beat it."

An hour later I was in a spirited battle in a Lake Forest basement with my archenemy D. Quail. After a particularly long and retarded battle, I emerged victorious and I ordered my conquest to go and get the birthday boy a giant bouquet of balloons. Magically D. Quail found some stashed in the adjacent hallway. Quail delivered them to the birthday boy and then we began a rousing version of our happy birthday song. As the moment we were supposed to say the birthday boy's name approached, panic struck me. I had forgotten his name, and it wasn't coming to me. As we sang the third line of the song, I prayed Adam remembered his name. No going back now. Time slowed. My voice dropped down to that familiar inaudible tone I relied on while singing and Adam's voice confidently rose above mine. I heard Adam, a cappella now, blurt out "Happy birthday, dear Tony." It was then that I remembered the boy's name was Kevin.

The next day Gail called and informed me that the clients in Lake Forest thought Ba-Looney Tunes employees were jerks. She suggested I drive to Evanston to return my costumes. I had failed Gail. I was a jerk.

When I got to Seth and Gail's house, Seth was not around. It seemed right that Gail and I have our farewell alone. We were the ones who had a relationship. Gail had me leave the helium tank on the driveway and bring everything else into the living room so she could check it off her inventory list. I stood there silently as Gail went through the boxes of my former career. I kept my eyes on Gail's fetish chair off in the corner. If Gail couldn't watch people sing, then I couldn't look at people who were firing me. As Gail cut the check for the money she owed me, minus $25 for the bow and suction cup arrows Crazy Rick had broken on Michelangelo's back, she offered me this parting advice: "You know, doing singing telegrams is just like doing stand-up comedy. You have to like it to be good at it." She was right. I was awful at both. Shortly afterward I sat in a chair facing my living room wall and fired myself from stand-up comedy.

Matt Walsh has never donned the Love Assassin's costume again, but he is a founding member of the Upright Citizen's Brigade, starred in the movie *Old School,* and was a regular cast member of *The Daily Show.*

GRRL GENIUS GETS CANNED

Cathryn Michon

I wanted to be Carol Burnett, so I spent a lot of my youth practicing pulling my ear in the mirror. I also memorized all of Lily Tomlin's routines, you know, in case she needed backup. For some reason the networks never pulled me off the school bus and whisked me off to Hollywood.

So naturally I had all sorts of nonshowbiz jobs. I worked at a clothing store called Mary Adams in the HarMar Mall, which was kind of like the Taj Mahal of Roseville, Minnesota. I did pretty well there but the situation got a little sticky for me when they asked me to compete to be Miss HarMar Mall and I didn't want to. I saw it as a dead-end coronation. The previous year's Miss HarMar Mall still lived in town and worked as assistant manager at Walgreen's.

So I took stock of my situation and realized that to get ahead I needed to find a job closer to show business, so I started waiting tables at a deep-dish pizza restaurant in Chicago. Everything was going pretty well until I dropped a deep-dish pizza on a guy wearing an Armani suit. I knew it was an Armani because he kept repeating over and over, "You dropped a deep-dish pizza on my Armani," though the weird thing was he put the emphasis on the word "deep." My manager came over and fired me on the spot: Apparently there was something in the employee manual about not dumping food on expensive menswear. He said, "You can go." And guess what: I wanted to go! I turned in my apron right there. Later, though, in my mind, I rewrote the scene so that I asked the guy, "So do you think if it had been a thin-crust pizza, you'd be okay with it?" Rewriting dialogue, that turned out to be something I was good at, so I went to work on a television show as a staff writer.

I got fired from that job too, though—and it had nothing to do with pizza of any kind. Actually the whole staff was fired. I got the call on Christmas Eve. My family had rented a house on the beach in Mendocino and I had spent some of my big TV money on presents and the phone rang with the news. No one in my family could believe I was working for the kind of people who would fire you on Christmas Eve; it was worse than the pizza business. But I wasn't actually that hurt. Somehow it helped that everyone had been fired. It's not as bad when the whole ship sinks as when it's just you being thrown overboard. Besides, they told me it was actually a good thing. Those were the exact words: "This is actually a good thing." I still have no idea what they meant by that. Because what, it would be charac-ter-building for me? It would teach me to manage my money because I wouldn't have any?

So I went out to tell my parents I'd been fired, and I told them it was a good thing, and naturally they asked how the hell that could be, and I was forced to come up with something on the spot, which helped me on the path to declaring my genius. I said I was learning to deal with rejection. It's often said "rejec-tion is just protection" and the life of this grrl genius has been chock-full of protection. I've had more protection than Tony Soprano.

So that's how I handled it. I declared myself to be a grrl ge-nius and that this rejection just cleared the way for other things.

People say to me, "Cathryn, if I declared myself to be a genius with no evidence whatsoever, wouldn't I be in denial?" To which I say, "Yes, that's the whole idea! Denial is one of the most powerful tools available to us today in self-improvement.

Denial is just a negative word for positive thinking." If you get fired, just tell yourself that your ex-employer doesn't deserve your genius! In truth every firing has been a "good thing" or a dreaded "growth experience" for me. Certainly, following every job I was fired from, I went on to do something if not better at least different and potentially more interesting. Still, always carry Godiva pastilles in your purse in case of an emergency firing. Chocolate helps.

Cathryn Michon is the author of the Grrl Genius books.

FIRED FACT

Sometimes an entire country wants to see you fired. On September 1, 2005, in the aftermath of Hurricane Katrina, with thousands trapped in the Superdome and Convention Center, FEMA director Michael D. Brown made the now infamous pronouncement, "Things are going relatively well." He resigned his position on September 12.[11]

Subject: All Those Parts
From: Your Mother
Date: March 1, 2004, 8:00 A.M., EST
To: firedbyannabellegurwitch.com

In 1956, right after I finished college, I had to earn money because my best friend Sandy and I were planning a road trip across the country to celebrate our graduation. I got a job working for the Air Force in the 82nd Material Squadron Base Supply. I was supposed to order airplane parts, but there was little training, and the files were so confusing. Everything was on little cards. So many cards! I wasn't sure which parts were in stock and I never saw any parts come in. I figured it was better to have a few extra of everything, right? So I spent every day back-ordering airplane parts. Really, I had no idea what I was doing.

I was so sure I was going to get fired, I quit right before all the orders started arriving. I told them I was moving to California so they wouldn't try to track me down!

But I had made the money for the trip. We went to the Corn Palace in South Dakota, the Grand Canyon, everything. It was the biggest thing that had happened to me in my life. We had adventures! I remember we went to the Top of the Mark in San Francisco, but unescorted women were not allowed in the better cocktail lounges in San Francisco and the maître d' asked us to leave. Then these two guys bought us drinks and one of them said his father was the mayor of San Francisco but he wasn't. That's a whole other story! You know, it was a long trip from Delaware to California and back, and every once in a while, as we would drive past a cornfield, I would think, I hope they have room on the airfield for all those parts!

Chapter 4:

The Time Getting Fired Leads You to Something Better

All great success comes from failure and being fired is part of the growth process. I mean, if we're not getting fired, what are we doing?

Robert Reich, secretary of labor 1993–1997

By working faithfully eight hours a day you may eventually get to be a boss and work twelve hours a day.

Robert Frost

Getting fired is God's way of telling you that you should be doing something else.

playwright Stephen Adly Guirgis

PATRICIA HEATON
HOPES YOU ENJOY YOUR STAY

One of the first people to tell me their story about being fired was Patty. Maybe it was the several margaritas I had that night, but after hearing her story, I did start to feel better.

Annabelle: Patty, what kind of jobs did you have before you started working as an actress?

Patty: I sold plasma in college for drinking money. I'd come out plasmaless and get legless. I was also a crossing guard. I had wanted to be in a sorority and I had to pay for it. I got fired from that job for chronic lateness. My boss was like the Robert Duvall character in *Apocalypse Now:* "If you're late, you're out." I was just doing the job to earn enough to pay for my sorority, so once I had made enough, I found I just couldn't get out of bed at six A.M.

Annabelle: He didn't say, "I love the smell of napalm in the morning"?

Patty: We had an understanding. He said he had to let me go as I was already handing him back my vest and flashlight.

Annabelle: What other jobs did you do?

Patty: I was working for a company called Deposums; you'd read a hundred-fifty-page document and then summarize it. Once I had been up all night doing a proofreading for a Japanese ball bearing company and I accidentally deleted the entire document. I found out something about myself that really serves me well today. I shut down emotionally

and deeply buried my anger and disappointment
and redid the document. This particular ability has
served me well as an actress and a mother. I also
worked at a lot of restaurants. I usually had about a
six-month window before I couldn't work there
anymore.

Annabelle: What would happen?

Patty: Boredom. Maybe subconsciously I didn't want to
get too comfortable. I got fired when I was managing a restaurant called Downtown. I had been
working there about six months when my back
went out. I got hives and I started coming in looking unwashed and depressed, and I was the person
greeting people at the door! I remember once
there was a guy leaning against the bar who was
clearly madly in love with whoever he was with and
I was staring longingly at them. He took my hand
and he said something like "Don't worry, it's going
to be okay." It's really not good when you have to
talk the hostess off the ledge.

Annabelle: How did the management fire you?

Patty: The owner, Philip, made me do all the work at the
end of the night, and then he handed me an envelope. Now, I was close friends with his girlfriend,
and I had worked there for six months, and he said
to me, "That's all we'll be needing from you." I
didn't know what he meant, so he said, "You don't
need to come back." I was really freaked out. I had
no money. It was really scary. But I also felt relieved. I don't think I was ever fired again.

Annabelle: Do you feel you use any of your hostessing skills as
an actress?

Patty: I always feel it's up to me to try to set the tone and atmosphere on the set and that's very hostessy. And show business is very political and restaurants are very political.

Annabelle: In what way do you think they are alike?

Patty: You have to know your place on the food chain.

Annabelle: So would that be your best quality as an employee?

Patty: I suck up well.

Annabelle: Give me an example of a good suck-up.

Patty: When you work for a network, you get a minimum of four gifts a year that are rendered useless because they have the corporate logo on them so when they come, you don't even bother to unwrap them. I always call each person from the head of the network down and thank them for sending me the CBS blanket/picture frame/bags/candle/basket/bathrobe. I call when I'm sure they'll be out—they don't really want to talk to me—just to make sure they know that I take nothing for granted in this business.

Annabelle: Is there a statute of limitations on a thank-you call? Once when I was on an HBO show I got a large something. It was a hammered pewter terrine. It looked like a shoe for an elephant. I didn't know what it was, so I never thanked them. That was Christmas 1989.

Patty: Not one executive has any idea if or what they sent you. Not only can you wait another year to thank them, you could call and thank them regardless of whether you received anything or not. And they would graciously accept your appreciation. In fact, it might be a good way to get a job. Call up every major executive and thank them for the lovely gift and they'll think that they are supposed to be in business with you.

Annabelle: Okay, what's your worst quality?

Patty: I memorize very quickly, and I learn everyone's lines. In the first year of *Raymond* I was reprimanded by a fellow cast member for prompting him with his line.

Annabelle: What did you do?

Patty: I was ashamed but I deeply buried my anger and humiliation and went on like nothing happened.

Annabelle: Have you ever been fired as an actor?

Patty: No, but I've been not hired.

Annabelle: Okay, what does it mean to you when your agent calls you after an audition and says, "They loved you."

Patty: Kiss of death.

Annabelle: "They're going a different way."

Patty: Air kiss of death. Once I was told, "Let me be honest, we're going with an attractive actress for this part."

Annabelle: Is there a job that you secretly covet?

Patty: Concierge. They're always helpful, friendly, they know where everything is, they get seats in restaurants, they always look so put together.

Annabelle: So if I don't see you again for ten years, I might go to the Four Seasons and I'll see you there and you'll say . . .

Patty: I hope you have a nice stay.

Patricia Heaton is the Emmy Award–winning star of *Everybody Loves Raymond*.

JIMMY THE IDIOT

Dana Gould

I never thought about getting fired. For years I made my living as a stand-up comedian, an occupation you can pretty much boil down to telling jokes in bars. You don't think about getting fired when what you do barely qualifies as a job.

Like most comedians, I figured it was only a matter of time before I segued into acting and achieved overnight global megastardom. After all I was a pretty good stand-up comedian. It stood to reason I would be a pretty good actor. Stand-up is all about talking, and acting is all about listening. See how similar they are? When it comes to listening to others, my motto has always been, "I have a better idea. What if I talk?"

In truth I was a terrible actor. Acting made me feel stiff, unnatural, and profoundly uncomfortable. This obvious pothole on my road to stardom concerned no one. Not me, and least of all my agent. Nothing concerned my agent, for, to him, I was not going to become just any old movie star. I was . . . the Next Robin Williams.

That's all I ever heard. "You're the Next Robin Williams. You're the Next Robin Williams." And why should I have doubted him? His car was much better than mine.

Unfortunately he would accept no job offer that consisted of anything less than my being instantly anointed the Next Robin Williams. A typical phone conversation would go as follows:

"Barry? It's Dana. The people from NBC want to meet me."

"Forget it. You're too good for them."

"But I'm unemployed."

"And when they're ready to rename NBC 'Dana Gould's

Good-Time Video Funhouse,' we'll call them back. In the meantime go home, lock your door, and hide under the couch. If people see you walking around during the day, you look too available and I lose bargaining leverage."

Did I really want to be the Next Robin Williams? Sure. I assumed it would be good for a grin. Plus I thought it would give me the leverage to write my own movies.

This is true. I figured I'd become a movie star and use it as a springboard to writing. Is there not a more difficult route? It was as if I wanted to be a pastry chef and entered politics to do it. After all, once I'm president of the United States, I can bake anything I want.

Eventually I realized this particular agent and I were not a very good match for each other and I fired him. Like a man. After an eighteen-month period of squirming and indecision.

Over time I learned how to act (sort of) and eventually found myself in a series of development deals. A development deal is where a studio or network matches a comedian up with an experienced TV writer in hopes they will create the next *Seinfeld* or *Everybody Loves Raymond*. The deal concludes with the shooting of a TV pilot.

Over the years I had my hand in more pilots than an Air Force proctologist. None of them worked, and I eventually got so fed up, I just wrote one by myself. I found the process rewarding and pleasurable. When that pilot didn't sell as a series, I was somewhat relieved, thinking that at least I didn't have to act in it.

I had an epiphany. "Aha!" I said aloud. "I'll become a writer. I can still be funny and, unlike with acting, I won't have to wear makeup."

Then the phone rang. My (new) agent wanted to know if I

would like to audition for a new show on NBC called *Working*, starring Fred Savage of *The Wonder Years*. I said, "No, I do not." In fact I told him right then and there that I wanted to shift the entire focus of my career to writing.

My agent told me that the director was a fan of mine and specifically requested me. Won't I please just audition? I said, "Look, I've never, ever, ever gotten a role off an audition. I'm no good at it. I walk into the room, forget everything I've ever learned, and run out two minutes later, naked, crying, and holding my clothes in a pile. I am putting my foot down. No."

I audition. And because, for the first time in my life, I did not care, because I did not give a rat's ass, I got the job. I am finally a working actor. All it took was a decision to quit acting.

The character I was to play was named Jimmy Clark, and that's pretty much all the character they had for this guy. In the script Jimmy Clark was more or less a head that popped up out of nowhere, fired off inconsequential one-liners when needed, then vanished back behind a filing cabinet. He never did anything, he just popped in and out, functioning as some sort of comedic prairie dog.

This weakness in the script is how I got the job. I brought a character in with me. Jimmy Clark became my old agent—well dressed, well groomed, loud, vacuous, and arrogant. In other words, a real person. Not someone you'd want to know, but someone you probably do know.

My first day at the show I walked into the wardrobe department expecting to find a bunch of slick, "agenty" suits, and instead found a purple shirt with an orange tie, checked pants, and golf shoes. Jimmy Clark had one joke in the script and it was about not knowing what a telephone was.

At some point, between the audition and the show, my character changed from a smug blowhard to a man with Down syndrome. I'm not Jimmy Clark, I'm Jimmy the Idiot. This is not what I signed up for. I don't need this. I could be home writing right now, in my own clothes and with no makeup.

I angrily marched down to the producer's office. For the sake of this story, we'll call him the producer. I'm going to tell the producer that I want to play Jimmy Clark like I did in the audition—like a real person.

As I neared the office, a voice in my head reminded me that I was being paid a great big pile of showbiz money and that maybe I shouldn't make any waves.

Thinking it over, I agreed with me and turned around. Back in my dressing room, I grabbed my ridiculous outfit and suited up.

Good thing. Because in the second episode of the show I was smart again. A math genius, in fact. In the third episode I was a motocross racer, and in the fourth episode I was back to being dumb, this time replaced by a chimp, but nobody noticed.

Alas, there never was a Jimmy Clark. He was whatever they needed him to be that week. I'm sure had I stayed with the show long enough, I would have eventually played a weather front. It would have been my big Emmy shot. Fred Savage is in a ski lodge, and Jimmy Clark is the wisecracking blizzard that won't let him get to the surprise party.

The show finished its first season and got picked up for a second. I was bored and frustrated, but I did have that big pile of money. I figured I'd take that big pile and buy my parents a house. It was a part of my lifelong desire to hear my father say those three little words, "Son, you win."

I bought them a house and figured I'd just make all my money next season. What could go wrong?

The phone rang. It was the producer, calling to say that the people at the network didn't feel that Jimmy Clark worked on the show. I'm very excited, because finally we agree on something. "Maybe," I trilled, "we could go back to the original—"

He interrupted, "So we're not going to have you back this year."

I was surprised, but I did summon up enough composure to inquire, "Go fuck myself?"

The producer, displaying the comedic sensibility that led him to create a character whose only consistent trait was that he occupied space and had mass, responded, "How do you think I feel? I have to make these calls."[1]

In retrospect, he did me a favor. By prying my mouth off the sitcom teat, he forced me to return to my nascent writing career. And if you're wondering how it all turned out, try to imagine the truckload of moolah they dumped on me for this little scribble.

A couple of years ago I was hired by a studio to write a movie. It was a coming-of-age story, not unlike *American Graffiti*, and I was very proud of it. When the studio read it, they loved it too. They only had one little adjustment. I blocked out what it was exactly, but it had something to do with changing the story to that of a horny robot that joins a fraternity.

After bitching and moaning to my wife about "the idiots in charge," etc., etc., I prepared to swallow my dignity and start typing, when the little voice returned, saying, "Jimmy the Idiot. Remember Jimmy the Idiot."

And so the next day I marched into the movie producer's office. This time I was not cowed by my paycheck, for I knew that road led to oblivion. I told the movie producer in no uncertain terms that I felt he was making a mistake. "Look," I called down from my high horse, "at the end of the day it costs the same amount of money to make a good film as a bad one. Let's make the movie we'll be proud of."

And that's how I got fired from that job.

Dana Gould is now a writer and producer of the award-winning show *The Simpsons*.

FIRED FACT

Nice work if you can get it! And getting fired can be fun if you have a spectacular severance package:

Conseco founder Stephen Hilbert: $72 million.[2]

Leonard Schaffer, WellPoint CEO who had a "constructive termination": $37.5 million plus country club membership, financial counseling, and office space and secretarial staff for five years.[3]

Philip Purcell, chief executive at Morgan Stanley: $113 million, medical benefits, and an administrative and secretarial staff for life.[4]

Carly Fiorina, chief executive of Hewlett-Packard: $21 million. Details of the packages of the over 15,000 employees terminated on her watch are unavailable; shortly after she departed, HP announced 14,500 job cuts.[5] You have to pay for that severance package somehow. . . .

THE WORLD'S WORST WAITER

Jeff Kahn

If I was ever your waiter, you had precious little time to witness my complete ineptitude, unmistakable frustration, and ill-mannered contempt before I was inevitably fired. I was the world's worst waiter. I was living in Chicago and became a waiter to support my addiction. At the time I was addicted to a terrible narcotic known as "acting." Acting, and wanting to act, make you do crazy things to support your acting habit. I happened to be hooked on one of the most addictive forms of acting—theater. Theater pays next to nothing and so it forces the user to do just about anything to get his fix. Although my need to act was boundless, I graduated from college with a BA in history with an emphasis on peasant anarchist movements in pre–Civil War Spain, which meant I entered the real world qualified to do two things: be unemployed or wait tables.

My first waiting job was at the River Club, a members-only restaurant that catered to Chicago's downtown business community in and around the Mercantile Exchange. The restaurant boasted dramatic views of the Chicago River. Out the floor-to-ceiling windows you could witness the majesty of Chicago's two climatic seasons: arctic and too fucking hot. I worked the lunch shift, which gave me plenty of time to concentrate on my first Chicago theatrical acting fix, the Sam Shepard play entitled *Geography of a Horse Dreamer*. I was cast as "Bell Boy." I had no lines. At the end of the play I came onstage, ignored the four dead bodies on the ground, and then for reasons known only to the playwright and perhaps Jessica Lange, switched on a zydeco record. I stood there silently as the lights dimmed. Makes no sense, I know, but I was a junkie and those brief, wordless minutes of stage time got me through a whole week's worth of waiting tables at the River Club.

To be a good waiter at the River Club you had to be efficient, friendly in a businesslike manner, and confident in your presentation and service. We served in the French style, which means something about talking from the left and serving from the right—I didn't know then and I don't know now. Rules like where to place plates and when to remove forks didn't really register with me because I was too busy daydreaming about acting in my next play—*The Memorandum*, written by Czech activist and playwright and future president Vaclav Havel. I must have been daydreaming when I accidentally dropped a tray loaded with entrees of pork tenderloin and pasta Alfredo. As the plates of food fell to the floor and broke, spilling a tidal wave of cream sauces and hog meat, I racked my mind to come up with the most efficient, friendly-in-a-businesslike-manner, and confident-in-my-presentation way to react to the situation. Yet all I could come up with was to scream, *"Fuck me!"* at the top of my lungs. I was fired on the spot.

Luckily I had *The Memorandum*. I was cast as "Office Spy," a character who spends the entire play unseen behind an office wall. I needed a new waiting job to pay for it—the Halstead Street Fish Market. This upscale fish restaurant served over twenty varieties of fish. Everything from the regal, steaklike tuna to the humble cod. And as with any addiction, I required more to get off, so while I pretended hard to give a shit about fish, I spent my off-hours searching back alleys and side streets for more acting. I found it at the Victory Gardens Theater's adaptation of Samuel Beckett's play *Catastrophe*. I was "Man on a box wearing a shroud." For the entire duration of the play I stood on a box wearing a shroud. People in the audience would ask me later what I was thinking about up there on that box, and

I told them, "I was thinking, why do I keep getting these horrible acting parts?" One night, in desperate need of protein, I was caught by the owner of Fish Market in the men's room scarfing down a customer's half-finished "catch of the night"—trout almandine—and I was sacked yet again.

Desperate, unemployed, and on a powerful acting jones, I decided to hit up my famous friend John Cusack. Not wanting to be outdone by his tall, limo-left-wing movie star friend Tim Robbins, who had a theater in L.A., John launched his own theater in Chicago by presenting the play *Alakazam*, written by Tim. The play was a forerunner of HBO's *Carnivàle*, about a traveling carnival freak show in the 1940s. Of course I was paid nothing, so I had to get yet another waiting job. I scored on the top floor of the windowless Water Tower Shopping Mall, in a deli theme restaurant called D. B. Kaplan's. Waiters were required to memorize more than two hundred sandwiches, of which I could remember only the "Jim McMahon," the "Oprah," and "Mrs. O'Leary's Cow," and the waiters were required to keep and make their own change. At the end of the night, when we cashed out, whatever money we had over the gross amount of the totaled checks, we kept as tips. Besides being painfully inefficient and easily flustered as a waiter, I also completely suck at math. Night after night, the money I had in my pocket was less than the totaled checks. I was, in effect, losing money by working. In order to keep acting, pay rent, and subsidize my D. B. Kaplan's job, I took on a second, part-time job passing out flyers for the Sex Shop on Wells Street.

During one frantic lunch rush at D. B. Kaplan's I scalded my hand ladling a bowl of cheddar cheese soup. One of the chefs, and by chefs I mean a guy who makes sandwiches and calls waiters, regardless of their sex, "she," "her," and "you little girl," sadistically laughed at me as I held my cheese-scorched hand under cold water. "Did *she* get burned? Did the poor *little girl* burn *her little girl* hand?" I lost it. I took a knife and pointed it at him. "And so what if she did?" I said. "So what if she did?" He immediately grabbed his much bigger, much sharper kitchen knife and began screaming threats at me, which I have every belief he intended to carry out. He wouldn't back off until the managers agreed to fire me, which they did. Interestingly, during the same short time I was at D. B. Kaplan's, Andy Dick was also working there. There were rumors that Andy was actually a worse waiter than me. He gave food away free to friends in front of paying customers and hit on underaged tourists, but who was a worse waiter I guess is a debate for the ages. Meanwhile I had a play to act in. My character in the play *Alakazam*, Lenny Roostman, the half man, half chicken, wore a chicken suit made out of a pair long underwear covered with real chicken feathers. In the stifling heat of summertime Chicago my sweat turned the chicken suit into a hardened shell of stale, dried perspiration that grew stiffer and more malodorous as the run of the play went on. "What kind of life is this?" I asked myself. How many more restaurant jobs did I need to be fired from to realize I'm not really a food service type of guy? The truth was, it wasn't waiting tables that was turning me into a freak, it was acting.

Thankfully that was all a long time ago and I'm happy to report I've been "acting-free" for years. Of course if a friend calls and offers me a part in a TV show or film, I take it. But c'mon, if I don't have to audition for it, it's no big deal, right? And I do these funny characters I make up for my five-year-old son, but I only do them long enough to make him laugh or scream, "Stop it, Daddy, you're bothering me!" Yet, and I can't stress this enough, it's not like I still dream of some casting director making a mental note to herself to call me in the next time she's looking for someone who's an odd mix of Roger Daltry and Gene Wilder. Okay, fine, so I'm still addicted. Acting is harder to quit than heroin. Fortunately I no longer have to wait tables to support my habit. I'm a writer. It's a lot more precarious than waiting, but the benefits are better and I have yet to burn my hand on a computer keypad.

Jeff Kahn is an Emmy Award–winning writer from *The Ben Stiller Show*. He does appear in the film *40 Year-Old Virgin* and yes, it was him playing a desperate actor working as a clown in *Entourage*.

FIRED FACT

A single, surprising phone call and it was over. That's how Pierce Brosnan says he learned that his services as James Bond would no longer be required. "One phone call, that's all it took!" He says that before they stopped negotiations, the producers had invited him back for a fifth time.

His departure from the role was a "titanic jolt to the system," says Brosnan, followed by "a great sense of calm."[6]

Subject: I'll Knock Your Block Off
From: Andy Dick
Date: October 4, 2005, 1:34 A.M., PST
To: firedbyannabellegurwitch.com

Jeff doesn't know what he's talking about! It's true that I got fired from D. B. Kaplan's, but I wasn't a waiter.

I worked behind the counter putting orders into bags, poured the soup, and did deliveries. When I'd go out to do deliveries, I would stop by my agents' office and hold up my head shots to remind them who I was, and I'd take people's food with me to my auditions, so I was always late with the orders. But I didn't get fired for that. I got fired for giving away food to friends and people who were deserving. There was a girl who worked across the mall at the Gap folding clothes, and she was gorgeous. I would just watch her all day. She would come in for soup. One day I was giving her the soup, and I was leaning over the counter to smell her, and I said, "Just take it, it's on me," and I got caught red-handed. The manager made me follow him to the back room where the time cards were and he fired me. He said, "Punch out your time card, you're fired! Get out and if you ever show your face here again, I'll knock your block off!"

I actually ended up dating that girl, but that's a story fraught with nights of sweaty passion and chlamydia. Months later my parents came to visit me in Chicago and they wanted to go to D. B. Kaplan's. My dad was insistent. He really wanted the Reuben sandwich from D. B. Kaplan's, and I said, "We can't go there, or he's going to knock my block off!" Of all the things I've done in my life, I think not being able to get my dad that Reuben sandwich may be the thing that's disappointed him the most. Still, I really owe my career to working at D. B. Kaplan's. That's where I met Jeff. He introduced me to Ben Stiller, who hired me to do his show on Fox, and that was my first really big break in show business.

Andy Dick's credits include *The Ben Stiller Show, News-Radio, Less Than Perfect,* and his eponymous MTV show, where he got a chance to fire others.

FIRED FACT

In 2004, Mikhail Baryshnikov said, "I was fired from an acting job. The theater director kindly said that I was not ready. He wrote a nice well-written letter. That's one way to do it. The Donald has his way."[7]

BOB SAGET
DOESN'T SIT HERE ANYMORE

1986. The renowned executive producer Bob Shanks, the man who had started *Good Morning America* and had written the TV communications school required reading *The Cool Fire*, had been chosen by CBS to launch an innovative new morning program entitled *The Morning Program*.

The hosts of the show were the talented actress Mariette Hartley and former WOR news anchor Rolland Smith. Mark McQueen was hired to be the weatherman–slash–music personality interviewer, and I was crowned "sidekick," a term unused in morning television since they had had a chimpanzee on the *Today* show. Bob picked me off a tape with fifty other comedians that had been compiled by the William Morris Agency. He told me he would change my life, and he did. All for the better, no sarcasm intended.

I was to make my own comedy videos as often as budget and timing would allow. I also introduced new comedians in the "Comedy Corner" segment—bringing on a pre-sitcom Roseanne, interviewing Benny Hill, and attempting my own comedy bits between seven and nine every weekday.

All was going well. Getting home from the show was my own matter, but every morning I was picked up in a town car at my apartment on the Upper West Side. Once I was even flown from New York to Los Angeles on a private jet with William S. Paley, Gene Jankowski, Tom Lahey—all veteran, well-established CBS chiefs. A seventy-year-old butler on the flight had cut the crust off the bread on my sandwiches. I was on the way to success.

For about four months I had made comedy videos, utilizing all the equipment and lighting CBS would allow me to smuggle into locations around Fifty-seventh Street. Then one day Bob told me I'd have to curtail my shoots. The videos were getting too costly, and not all of them were working. That was the truth, I guess.

One morning a few days after being told my video shoots were being reined in, I showed up to work on time, about 5:30 A.M., and . . . my hosting chair was gone. Just Mariette's and Rolland's were there. Bob saw me looking at the empty chair space and told me, "We're gonna try to get your chair back." But it didn't return. I was relegated to sitting on the steps in the studio, among the audience members, doing the off-camera announcements: "It's fifteen minutes after the hour . . ." I still had a couple of on-camera moments, an intro here or there, but it was obvious I was getting phased out. It went on for probably a week.

I was called up to Bob's office with my manager, Brad Grey, who was in town. I told Bob I wasn't happy with how it was working out. He told me it was mutual; it wasn't working out for the CBS brass either. The network felt I was "too hot for morning TV." It was a nice way of letting me down, kinda sorta. "Too much energy, too edgy . . ." "You truly cannot scare the more middle-of-the-road viewers. They pay the bills." So I was asked to leave. Bob Shanks was incredibly nice about it. He'd had to clip my wings throughout my on-air decline, and in a way I think my leaving was an indication to him that his dream morning show was now deteriorating.

The network gave the show four more months. Then they canceled it for good and took the seven-to-nine-A.M. time spot away from the entertainment division.

I had a couple of weeks to pack and return to Los Angeles, where I'd secretly screen-tested for a pilot for this family show called *Full House*. The whole exercise might've been a violation of my CBS contract, if my firing hadn't been imminent. I had just had a baby and spent a lot of our money to live in New York, so I really needed another job. Brad made a call and found out they had wanted me for *Full House* from the beginning. Since I wasn't available, the producers had shot the pilot with another actor. I would replace him, and they would reshoot the pilot with me as the straitlaced nice guy, widowed father of three girls. With a new baby in my arms, I signed a five-year deal. I considered it a gift.

I never thought I would work again. And that was three months ago.

No, I mean after the *Morning Program* experience. But I will never forget that show and I will always appreciate it. I had moved out to New York from L.A., I had lived on the Upper West Side, and I had had a ride to work. Not a ride *home* from work, but it was only a thirty-block walk. I have nothing but gratitude for Bob and Anne Shanks. I think they genuinely thought I was funny and genuinely felt bad when it didn't work out.

I've been fired only a couple of times in my life, and my firing from *The Morning Program* was marked by the least passive-aggressive behavior that I've ever dealt with in my career. I was just taken into an office and told "it wasn't working out." That's how you fire a man in show business. I didn't have to read about it in *Variety*. For that I will always be appreciative. I did read about another job of mine "not working out" in *Variety*, but that's for the next book . . .

Bob Saget starred in the sitcom *Full House* from 1987 to 1995 and hosted *America's Funniest Home Videos* from 1989 to 1997. He has recently appeared in *The Aristocrats* and on *Entourage* on HBO. Bob's fans are so fanatical about him that there are Web sites devoted to proving that Bob Saget is God. He is an active supporter and fund-raiser for the Scleroderma Research Foundation.

FIRED FACT

Number of times George Steinbrenner hired Billy
   Martin to be the Yankees' manager: 5
Number of times Steinbrenner fired Martin: 5[8]

CAN YOU GET FIRED
IF YOU AREN'T BEING PAID?

Morgan Spurlock

One of the worst jobs I ever got fired from wasn't a job at all: I was free labor on a movie! I was working for nothing on a no-budget film, right after I got out of film school.

It was after lunch and they had just started shooting a scene in the bedroom, so I'm sitting on an apple box, being quiet in the other room because they were shooting and I fell asleep against the wall. The producer wakes me up and tells me to go home: If I'm not going to help, they don't need me anymore. Don't need me? I'm *free labor*! You need all the help you can get! What are you talking about? The producer said I was a bad influence on the rest of the crew. Oh, you mean the *rest* of the *free labor* crew? The producer said, and I'll never forget this, "I'm not paying you to sleep." I laughed. "You're not paying me at all!" Moron. So I picked up my jacket, walked out of the apartment building, past the PA who was *sleeping* in the grip truck, and went home. Actually I woke up the PA when I went past and told him, "If you want to keep this job you're not getting paid for, then you better stay awake." Needless to say I never used that producer as a reference and was very excited to see him eight years later—serving coffee in a local Starbucks.

Morgan Spurlock is the director of *Super Size Me.*

I WAS THE MASTER

Tim Allen

During my second year of college at Central Michigan University in the lovely hamlet of Mount Pleasant, Michigan, I was working at a place called the Light Factory, a disco. It had a neon floor that moved and lit up. It was the first one in the country. You danced on Plexiglas. I was the deejay. I had my own drummer, tight jeans, and free shitty drinks. It was a dream job. I was playing Earth, Wind & Fire and the J. Geils Band. I also had a beard and long hair and looked like Jim Morrison on a bad day. I think I got five dollars an hour, but it wasn't about the money. I had a posse who would come to hang out and hear me. I've always loved setting up a party. I could raise it to a fever pitch with "September" and and bring it down with "Reasons"—you know, so the folks could rest and maybe slow-dance. I was the master!

The owner had four clubs and he asked me to manage the newest one. It was a real opportunity, a career even: We could have gone national. When I hesitated because I might "miss some classes," the owner was stunned. He said he'd never misjudged someone so much before, that I was younger and much less experienced than my persona. He was disappointed but he needed to hire someone and he ended up with a slick dick from New York. This guy had really permed curly hair and thought he was better than everybody else. Within a week he took me backstage and actually said with a straight face, "I'm going to let you go. You're talented, you've got creative ideas, and people like you. I hate popular people. You remind me of all the things I don't do well. I don't want to be reminded of my shortcomings." I have always admired the guy because he told his truth. I was fired and complimented on the same night. So I moved on and became just another average liberal arts student who loved comedy.

Tim Allen still loves throwing parties and has attended a lot of them himself, having hosted the Emmys and having won Golden Globes and People's Choice Awards. He starred in, wrote, and produced the popular series *Home Improvement*. He also starred in the *Toy Story* and the *Santa Clause* movies and is one of the most successful actors working in films today.

FIRED FACT

Richard Foos, cofounder of Rhino Records, recalls, "Right after college I was running a community organization. We gave clothing to people on welfare, so to subsidize that I got a job as delivery boy for a pharmacy. I had one week of training and got fired after maybe two weeks. I delivered the wrong drugs. The pharmacist just said, 'It's not working out.'

"The unbelievable thing was a week later I got a call from the pharmacist saying that he had accidentally paid me for the training week and wanted his money back.

"I said, 'Fuck you!' And I swore I'd never work for anyone ever again and I never have."

MADISON SCARE GARDEN

Elizabeth Warner

Growing up in the Protestant blood clot that is suburban Philadelphia—where one is weaned, whelped, and gently engineered to live snappily ever after—I'd never imagined that eleven dollars an hour and a reprieve from eviction would be worth risking imprisonment. Then again, I hadn't thought Radiohead, merlot, or Tibet would catch on in a big way either.

In 1999 I was so strapped financially that I secured a job—the only job I could find—whose sole requirement was my ability to show up. And in order to *maintain* my post as the witch of Madison Scare Garden's Halloween Scream Park, I actively and illegally evaded jury duty. And all it took was a bottle of Wesson oil and two quarts of soy sauce.

I managed to land the Madison Scare Garden witch job from a field of thirty other actors. As I entered the audition room, the casting director asked me simply to scream as maniacally as I could and then to present proof of U.S. citizenship, at which point I was cast.

The only key to keeping the job, we were told, was to actually show up. On the day I was hired, I happened to receive my second notice to serve on a jury. At the time I was hopelessly in love with a bright, grumpy journalist who had a serious Alan Arkin complex. The two of us were charitably referred to as the Jew and the shrew. He told me to ignore the jury summons because I was a working actor and that was the most important thing. Although, he said, in the end it wouldn't really matter, as all Protestants have a genetic predisposition toward that A. R. Gurney–type of proud decay and well-educated failure. But in the meantime I should take the job and keep it at all costs.

At our first rehearsal the seventy-five actors hired were shown around the vast expanse of the Garden. The show's producer was tireless and ultracharismatic—one of those people who really could inspire bitter, mismatched actors to freakish greatness daily. I quickly befriended an essentially topless dwarf who took me under her wing and explained that she did the straight white bonfire of commerce otherwise known as the Radio City Christmas Show every year—both in New York and regionally—and that she played elves and only elves, and that *she would never be caught dead playing one of them fuckin' faggot-ass panda bears.* I then asked her if she had an extra cigarette and she stared at me and said, "Well, they don't come twenty-one in a pack but I'll give you one," and I knew our bond was sealed.

The show ran from three o'clock in the afternoon until two o'clock in the morning, and the clientele mirrored these hours. By ten thirty there were no children, only cavorting teens, tipsy hoodlums, and silent, smirking people who had probably done time.

My assignment, my post, was "Scarewood Forest," which served as a haven for frightened children, a nursery, and a general area where I was instructed to roam and comfort children who were scared and scare children who looked comfortable. I was supposed to usher 146 people into the theater every fourteen minutes. I was frequently reminded to frighten as many people as I could, which given the amount of makeup, oozing sores, and latex on my face, was possible to do simply by asking an unsuspecting person the time.

During the first week three actors called in sick and were fired instantly. That same week I received another jury summons that arrived with an accompanying threat of "punitive action or imprisonment" if I failed to comply, followed by a letter ordering me to the courthouse. I panicked at this rock and hard place of just getting by. I couldn't afford not to work. I decided that it's better to show up for an awful job that pays you than to sit through an even more unpleasant one that doesn't. I devised a plan to get myself fired from jury duty.

Now, I'd been told that you could make outrageous claims that reflected bigotry or prejudice and be deemed unfit for jury duty. I'd had friends who had simply made remarks like "Neither foreigners nor Canadians can be trusted" or "I don't have a problem unless it's with the Puerto Ricans—they're so shifty" or blurted out the ever-popular "Who says the Indians were here first? Look how much they drink!" Unfortunately city court officers knew every trick in the book. So I took a white T-shirt and tore it down the middle as violently as I could, then let it soak overnight in two quarts of soy sauce. I combed Wesson oil through my hair and parted it in the middle. I borrowed a pair of pink tortoiseshell glasses from a seventh grader in my building and stepped on the lens so it was completely shattered within the frame. I spent a dollar on an XXXL chartreuse down parka. I took one of my father's old prescription pads from the Institute of the Pennsylvania Hospital, the psychiatric hospital where he had worked until his death four years prior, and wrote myself a daily prescription for 500 milligrams of the SSRI antidepressant Paxil. I then took the subway to the courthouse, having zipped the green parka up to my chin, trying not to asphyxiate myself with the smell of soy sauce.

At the courthouse I told the court officer I'd be more than delighted to serve on jury duty because I was fascinated with "the evil that men do." I also explained that it was frequently hard for me to focus, emotionally. I underscored this visually by keeping my genuine wandering eye at a ninety-degree angle to my nose the entire time. The guy was clearly disturbed about the fact that he could focus only on one eye, and as he squirmed uncomfortably in his seat, I noticed that he would shift his glance from one of my eyes to the other. As he asked me questions, I ended each sentence with an unintelligible mumble. When he inquired, I'd say things like "Nobody understands, because Everybody Loves Raymond Burr . . ." before laughing as maniacally as I could. I also punctuated my sentences with bad words and constantly ran my fingers through my hair at forty-five-second intervals, before staring longingly at my greasy fingertips. He asked if I was warm in my down parka and I replied that "it's always cold in New York, if you know what I mean . . . because it's all about the man."

When he asked what I did for a living, I replied, "Oh, stuff," before explaining that my lethargy was "probably due to some weird strain of Lyme disease because I was in contact with a lot of ticks last summer."

I explained that the doctors had given me these pills for my Lyme disease fatigue, and I presented him with the prescription. He commented that the doctor had the same name as me and I said that I knew that, and that he was the only doctor I'd been able to find in America who wasn't part of those pinko Stalinist HMOs that are ruining our land. I then asked him about his doctor and his feelings about those Communist HMOs and was told politely that he worked for the City of New York so that wasn't really an appropriate topic. He then closed my file and explained that perhaps I shouldn't serve on a jury this time around and that maybe I could come back once my Lyme disease cleared up.

I left the courthouse and headed into the subway, ignoring the looks of commuters and the shriveling of their noses as I came near them, reeking of soy sauce. I raced to the Garden, sat for two hours in makeup, and went off to my job, which was now—since I'd been fired from jury duty—blessedly secure. Even though I have a black heart and an empty life, I am not immune to the bounty of spectacle. I actually grew to enjoy Madison Scare Garden. I found I began to appreciate and almost rely upon the consistency of it all. There was the joy in seeing a kid shriek and then laugh, the deeply personal horror I felt when a kid cried and begged to go home. Still, the screams that accompany the seventy-fifth overturned Coke are as poignant and resonant as the first.

So sure, I'd broken the law, and sure, I'd shirked my civic duty so that I could keep a post which served no good for mankind whatsoever. But who wants to be one of twelve angry men when you can get paid to wear latex?

Elizabeth Warner is the author of *Ditched by Dr. Right,* from which this essay was excerpted. She lives in Los Angeles, where she regularly performs her essays at the Comedy Central Workspace.

FIRED FACT

Ezra Pound was fired after a year on the faculty of Wabash College in Crawfordsville, Indiana, in 1905, for befriending a transsexual. Or as they called it back then, a "lady-gent impersonator." Pound departed for Europe, where he would remain for most of his life.[9]

D. L. HUGHLEY:
LOT AND LOBBY TO LATE NIGHT

When I was sixteen I worked at McDonald's. I wore the whole uniform: blue pants, blue shirt with white shoulders, and a crisp paper hat. I was so proud of it that I would wear it to parties. Black women love a man in a uniform because it's proof that he's got a job! I worked there for six months and this is the truth: I never got to work the fry machine or to make a burger. They would never let me drop fries. My whole life I wanted to go, "Drop fry on two," and press that little red button, and then when it turns green, the fries are ready. I never got a shot at that. I only got to do "lot and lobby." I would clean the parking lot and lobby so good that people would leave me tips. You know that you're doing a good job when they tip you for that!

But I got fired, because this one time I came to work early, 'cause the lot was giving me *power trash* and I wanted to assess what tools I would need to make sure it was *clean*.

Well, this dude who worked there, he was my boy, he hooked me up—gave me a free Egg McMuffin. The manager called me into the office. He said, "Who gave you the Egg McMuffun?" I said, "Man, I'm not gonna tell you who gave me that." He said, "I know who did it, just tell me." I said, "If you know who did it, we should not be having this discussion." Egg McMuffins cost maybe seventy-five cents at the time. "If you don't tell me, you're fired," he says. Man, this was my job. I was proud of it. I said, "Then I guess I'm fired." He said, "You are." He took my paper hat and put me out the back door. For weeks I walked around in that uniform because I didn't want to tell my mom I got fired. I used to go hang out, pretend I was going to work. Eventually no money was rolling in and she figured it out.

Seventy-five cents! That dude, he was a brother, that mother-fucker could have hooked me up!

It's still hard for me to order an Egg McMuffin. When my children were little, they'd want to go to McDonald's. I'd wait in the car or walk around the lot and lobby and check it out and go, "This ain't really clean! I could have done so much better than this."

D. L. Hughley created and starred in the TV series *The Hughleys* from 1998 to 2002. He is the host of *Weekends at the DL* on Comedy Central.

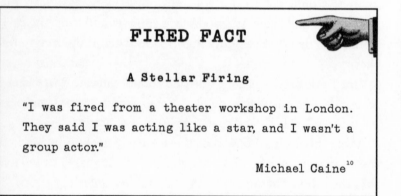

FIRED FACT

A Stellar Firing

"I was fired from a theater workshop in London. They said I was acting like a star, and I wasn't a group actor."

Michael Caine[10]

NO SHIRT, NO SHOES, NO SERVICE

Maxine Lapiduss

I started doing stand-up in Pittsburgh, when I was fourteen. I scored at the local clubs with my "Anybody here have parents?" schtick, and my signature "Here's what I don't get about baby-sitting" bit. As I developed—my act and my breasts—my dreams of fame and fortune took flight and I realized there was more to this business we call show than knocking 'em dead at Yuk-Yuks in Kittanning. Plus my college girlfriend, whom I was certain I would spend the rest of my life with, dumped me at graduation. Heartbroken, I headed to New York.

If I could just get on stage at the Improvisation or Catch a Rising Star, by the end of summer, I reasoned, I'd be a comedy sensation, landing multiple spots on *Letterman*. Once that happened, my two-timing girlfriend would realize what a *huge* mistake she'd made downsizing me from our relationship and beg me to come back.

I shot out of the Holland Tunnel and headed for Audition Day at the Improv.

I arrived to find Jews standing in long lines, praying, ranting, sleeping in the street: it was like a scene out of *Schindler's List*. Everyone was jockeying for a low number and working their connections; I couldn't get near the top forty. So I focused on my fallback career. Waitressing. I'd had tons of experience back home. Mondays, Wednesdays, and Fridays I served flaming kabobs with a flourish at Samrimi's Shish Kabob House, while Tuesdays and Saturdays I schlepped shellfish to drunken men in fezzes at Knights of Columbus dinners. Landing a lucrative server poe-sish in the Big Apple would be the easy part of my master plan.

Eastside, westside, all around the town, these vagabond shoes scoured every bar, pub, and sandwich shoppe from Columbus Ave to Restaurant Row. But I was too late.

It was June. All the summer jobs had been snapped up.

And I had frittered away all my savings on frivolous incidentals, like rent and shampoo.

Down to my last twenty-five bucks, I landed a job at the Saloon, a hot spot across from Lincoln Center, by lying. I claimed I could roller-skate.

The place had a series of ramps so you could traverse from kitchen to bar to outdoor patio effortlessly. That is, if you knew how to stop.

I borrowed some in-line babies from a pal and hit Central Park to practice. After two hours on those death machines, I had ten giant blisters where toes used to be and a softball-sized contusion on my hip from blading over a Nathan's hot dog. At least I hope it was a Nathan's hot dog.

My first four-top (that's waitress lingo) was a quartet of opera queens all of whom ordered fennel-tomato soup before the curtain of *Così fan tutte*. Tray aloft, I taxied to the runway, took a breath, rounded ramp one, and instantly hit a patch of mayo that greased the track like an oil slick. Skidding out of control, I bobbed and weaved, almost taking out a table of old folks before their time. I picked up steam by the steam table, and "Whoa!"-ed my way past the condiment bar, whizzing out the open door, where I was forced to make what would have been Sophie's choice had she been a waitress—burn every patron on the patio or use my own body as a human shield. I hugged the tray into my torso and crashed into the rail.

Bowls smashed to the ground and I, sprawled and scalded, lay in a river of my own blood. Actually it was just the fennel-tomato soup, but that doesn't sound as dramatic. Suffice it to say I wasn't asked back for the dinner shift.

I tapped my last bit of savings buying gauze and Neosporin. I was crippled and broke, physically and emotionally, not to mention completely humiliated.

It was the same feeling I'd have years later when Jeff Foxworthy fired me from his TV show for "creative differences," which I took to mean "for being funnier than he was." But all the writers were funnier than he was. The craft service lady was funnier than he was. It didn't help that I was a woman hired to run his ill-conceived show. And a Jewess to boot. Seriously. I would speculate that the last time he'd seen that many Jews sitting around a table, it was a painting of the Last Supper.

Oh, did I mention I was also a lesbian? When that tidbit came to light, I thought he'd have to be hospitalized. I'd put down cold, hard American cash that the closest he ever came to a lesbian was ogling a glossy girl-on-girl action spread in *Hustler*. Suffice it to say I was not his lesbian fantasy. But he was my redneck nightmare.

Meanwhile, as I looked for a waitressing gig, I was leeching money from my sister, Sally, who, as an out-of-work casting director, was leeching money from Unemployment.

Every day I'd make my rounds—

I marched into JR's on West Forty-sixth, for the third time, application in hand.

The manager, Lindy, a zaftig blond, must have liked my spunk, or sensed my physical dexterity at carrying multiple plates up my arm. Or perhaps it was the fact that I burst into tears in the midst of begging her for work. Whatever the reason, she said there might be an opening. She'd let me know soon. I left feeling certain that marrying ketchups would once again be in my future. That was Wednesday. Thursday came and went, then Friday, then a week . . . no call. About 6:30 the following Sunday I was at Sally's waiting for her to come home so she could take me for Chinese.

It was a million degrees outside and a million and ten in her apartment. Sweating profusely, I began to sob. My life was over. I had no lover, no career, no crappy waitress job, not even a dry T-shirt at this point. Ninety days in New York and I was a beaten woman.

It's up to you, New York, New York? Well, screw you, New York, New York. It's back to the Burg for this hacky no-talent. Back to shish-kabob central, reeking of baba ghanoush as I watch my ex-girlfriend sashay in with her patchouli-scented beauty, taunting me by feeding herself the grape leaves I've just served. Fuck! Well, at least I have my act. Which I'll perform . . . at the Red Barn Theater in Greentree or Temple Sinai Sisterhood luncheons? Jesus, criminy! God! Don't make me go back to Pittsburgh! Anything but that! I prayed and screamed and begged "Yaway" for "a little help here." For Christ's sake, "One freakin' waitress job—is that so much to ask? One sucky, shit-hole job that gets me a tuna melt for lunch and pays my half of the hellhole rent! I'm working my ass off! I'm a good person! I'm fucking grateful!" As I kept enumerating my bitchy deal points to the Guy Upstairs, the phone rang, interrupting me.

It was Lindy. I couldn't afford a phone of my own, so I'd given her Sally's number. Lindy said I could start the next morning at JR's. "Really?"

"Be here at ten thirty in black shoes, black pants, and a white shirt. See you then."

She hung up. Wow. In a flash, my prayer'd been answered.

I rinsed my swollen eyes and mentally ran through my wardrobe. I had black jeans and black shoes but no white shirt. Sally's shirts were too big for me. I'd be swimming in them. I looked through her roommate Alan's closet. His entire wardrobe was studded leather.

It was now 7:30. I walked toward Broadway. The streets were desolate; it was like a ghost town above Ninety-sixth Street on Sunday nights.

I entered Empire Szechwan Gourmet, not to be confused with Empire Szechwan Gourmet Jr., which was three doors down, or Empire Szechwan, which was one block up. Sal-Gal was already at our table with the cold sesame noodles and scallion pancakes. I brought her up to speed.

"Where are you going to get a white shirt at this hour on a Sunday night?" she asked. "Nothing's open up here."

"I have no freaking idea," I said.

I could feel my anxiety rising and the sickly, familiar feeling of doom in the pit of my stomach.

I'd report for work in a pink shirt or a plaid shirt and Lindy would become apoplectic. "Can't you do anything right, Lapiduss? Day one and you can't even look like a waitress? No wonder your girlfriend dumped you. You're pathetic. And you're fired."

"Oh, God," I chanted silently, "you gotta help me out here. If I'm supposed to stay in this crazy city, you gotta help me out here." Broadway was pitch-black, the street eerily quiet, as we headed toward our apartment. We rounded 106th and I could feel the tears begin to well up again. We hit Amsterdam and there, a few steps ahead of us, stood a lanky black dude, about thirty, in fatigues and a green army jacket.

He had laid out a ratty blanket on the pavement that held a few tattered comic books for sale. Above the stoop of the sagging building hung a laundry cord.

I looked up, and there hanging before me on that cord was a bevy of clean, crisp, white shirts blowing gently in the evening breeze. There had to have been, I'm so not kidding, forty white shirts. No beige, no cream, all pure white.

Sally and I looked at each other, our eyes wide in amazement. It was so odd and specific. We walked that block at least four times a day, every day, and this guy had never been there before. Who was he selling to? The streets were deserted.

"How much for the shirts?" I asked.

"Fifty cents each," he responded calmly.

He nodded at me purposefully and then I saw his eyes—green—dazzling like my Aunt Eileen's emerald necklace, shimmering in the darkness, catching the light.

Then he smiled—revealing sparkling orthodontia. Then I got it. This wasn't some homeless kook living in a cardboard box. This was an absolute 100 percent unadulterated Rasta male-model angel.

He radiated warmth, grace, and protection, all focused in my direction. I gulped and looked at my last two—well, Sally's last two—crumpled dollar bills. One would buy me a subway token and a Kit-Kat tomorrow. I handed him the other and pointed at two perfectly ironed white shirts. He handed me the shirts, his eyes never leaving my gaze.

Sally and I walked away speechless. We both realized we had just witnessed a profound act of God. Granted, it might not have been in the top five for all mankind, like parting the Red Sea or Moses' coming down the mount with the Ten Commandments, but it was a spiritual experience. No doubt about that.

I got home and tried on both shirts. They fit perfectly. I started at JR's the next morning. A week later I ran into Ken Ober, a comic I'd worked with who was a regular at the Improv.

He hooked me up and I passed the audition with flying colors. I became a featured act at the hottest club in town and worked five shifts a week at JR's, able to pay my rent and pursue my dream.

I never saw the White Shirt Angel again even though I looked for him every single day until I moved to L.A. years later. And no, my ex didn't come crawling back, and I didn't make a million bucks or become an instant hit on *Letterman*.

But foolishly that wasn't what I had asked God to do for me. I'd asked for a below-minimum-wage job and some costume assistance, and that's exactly what I got. Next time, I'll be more specific.

Maxine Lapiduss is a writer, producer, and performer and makes a heck of a brisket, just don't ask her to serve you. Her writing credits include *Ellen, Roseanne,* and *Dharma and Greg,* and she was one of the stars and producers of *Situation: Comedy* on Bravo.

FIRED FACT

If you're going to get fired, try to get axed in Canada, France, or Brazil. Employers in those countries offer the most generous severance packages.[11]

Subject: But We'd Love to Work with You Again
From: Judd Apatow
Date: October 2, 2005, 11:20 A.M., PST
To: firedbyannabellegurwitch.com

You are sitting at home, happy as can be, when the phone rings. The call is from a low-level executive at the network, the one who actually "gets" your show but has no power. He tells you that your show has been canceled and that the head of the network will be calling you later in the morning.

Translated, that means the head of the network doesn't want to absorb your initial rush of anger and hatred so he/she pussies out and has someone else tell you. The network head waits several hours and, after the proper cooling off period, calls to say how terrible they feel and that they would like to work with you again in the future. What they never realize is that your emotion doesn't subside for months, even years, so you always feel the need to tell them every detail of how badly they supervised and marketed your show, and then you go on to tell them how badly the network is run in general. They always thank you for your candid comments with a voice so calm you realize they are probably talking to you on a speaker phone in a room filled with other executives who are giggling as you cry your tears of depression and rage.

Afterward you pray that this network head will be fired. And the final indignity is that when he/she is finally fired, usually eighteen months later, you have moved on and you don't feel any joy in their termination. That is because you also heard about his/her golden parachute, a clause in his/her contract that pays him/her millions of dollars to go away. Come to think of it, network prez is a sweet gig.

Judd Apatow's directorial debut, *The 40 Year-Old Virgin,* has grossed more than $150 million worldwide. You might want your show to be canceled if Judd produces it, as most everything he produces becomes a classic. *The Ben Stiller Show* was canceled after Fox aired only twelve episodes; it won an Emmy Award for comedy-variety writing. The canceled *Freeks and Geeks* was nominated for an Emmy; it lasted seventeen episodes; *Undeclared,* canceled after only sixteen episodes, is now a popular DVD release.

FIRED FACT

Fired Up

"I was fired from a Pizza Hut in Arlington, Virginia. I was a hostess, and the manager said I didn't do enough side work—you know, filling up bottles of salt and pepper. But I think he was dating some (of the other female employees), and that was the real reason." Katie Couric[12]

My best firing happened on the day I had planned to give notice. I had received a job offer the night before, and so I was happy to see the personnel manager in my office when I arrived. He told me my services were no longer needed, and because I had been a loyal employee I was getting a substantial severance check. I pretended shock and remorse, cleaned out my desk, and started my new job the following Monday with money in the bank.

Lilly Anderson is a newspaper copyeditor in Fort Wayne, Indiana.

FIRED FACT

One of the most deceptive euphemisms for laying off employees: "rightsizing."[13] Originally used by IBM when it laid off thirty-five thousand employees in the early 1990s, the term is now regularly used to refer to the firing of large groups of employees.[14]

Chapter 5

The Time You Had to Fire Yourself

A man is a success if he gets up in the morning and goes to bed at night and in between does what he wants to do.

Bob Dylan

Most people work just hard enough not to get fired and get paid just enough money not to quit.

George Carlin

If hard work were such a wonderful thing, surely the rich would have kept it to themselves.

Lane Kirkland

A THOROUGHLY MODERN FIRING

Tonya Pinkins

The great African actor Avon Long told me once, you always have to be aware of your nuisance value, because your talent has to be worth your nuisance. In the case of *Thoroughly Modern Millie*, mine was not. I had just come off doing the Broadway production of *The Wild Party* with Toni Collette. It was a brilliant creative experience and a financial flop. I needed some fat, juicy ego meat to pick me up. I wished for it and I got it, an offer to re-create the role of Muzzy, which had been lovingly memorialized on celluloid by Carol Channing in *Thoroughly Modern Millie*. It was an opportunity to contemporize and sassify this not really immortal character.

My first clue that something was amiss should have been the fact that my hiring was caused by the firing of one of my all-time favorite performers, Yvette Cason. Yvette and I had done *Play On* at the Old Globe Theater and again on Broadway. Not only is she a phenomenal actress, she is one of the best jazz singers I have ever heard. When I wanted to learn to scat for my role in *Play On*, it was Yvette who coached me to become passable. My ego told me they couldn't be firing her because she was pregnant. I myself had been nine months pregnant in *Play On*. It could be done. No, that wasn't it. They wanted me, my talent, and my Tony Award. Yes, a hungry ego will lead you astray every time.

My second clue should have been that the La Jolla Playhouse is rumored to have been built on old Native American burial grounds. The Ancestors were truly unhappy with us. The production was pushed back for weeks because a major set component could not be built to fit in the theater. A techie fell from scaffolding and broke his back, and the atmosphere in the rehearsal room was conducive to walking the plank. The star Erin Dilley became ill during rehearsals; the star Pat Carroll became ill during production. I was ill through it all. Erin Dilley and I became fast friends. A wonderful actress who was creating the humanity to fill the cartoon that was Millie, she was exhausted and frustrated, feeling that she was on the verge of being fired, and her precognition came true the same day she said it to me.

Have I failed to talk about my part in the show? That's because there isn't much to say. The good part was that the wig and the costume were the finest of my career. I wore a hand-beaded, skintight mermaid gown with an ostrich feather tail and a cape lined with fat pink roses. My entrance was from a spiral staircase; think cheap New York apartment renovation, not Tara. When I was in the gown and the cape I could barely squeeze between the two railings. The spiral was so tight that the train would get caught and prevent my moving at all. But no matter, because the circulating doughnut penthouse set piece blocked out the entire lower half of me and the fabulous gown. But it gets better. My two showstopping numbers were just that: showstopping. They didn't move the story onward and they simply lay there like rotten eggs, to quote a review. One was an original, entitled "You Were Born and Then What, Baby?" which was my question exactly because this tune went nowhere. The second, "Jazz Baby," was from the original movie, a real dud that Carol Channing had put her stamp on. My improvisational skills are minimal, though I have listened to the greats and can imitate a riff or two, but in this song I simply had nowhere to move vocally. I remembered Yvette telling me she turned "Jazz Baby" "out"; I simply begged for it to be *out* of the show.

I sat down with the creative team and shared all my creative thoughts: Muzzie as a black woman simply hadn't been justified and the first song didn't say anything that moved the story. I told them I'd rather have no number instead of a bad number like "Jazz Baby."

Although no one said the F word, I knew what it meant when I got the call to check my address so they could send my buyout fee. My only recompense was that by the time *Millie* got to Broadway, they had taken my advice on many counts. They had cut the set and cut the songs that didn't work. The show took home six Tony Awards, but of course they had cut me too.

And though the embarrassment of being fired is hard to swallow, I just think of Patti Lupone and her Andrew Lloyd Weber memorial swimming pool in honor of being fired from *Sunset Boulevard*. I simply buy myself the most expensive bauble my buyout can buy and remind myself that I am worth it.

Tonya Pinkins has been the recipient of one Tony Award and three Tony nominations in addition to her many other awards, including the Obie, Drama Desk, Outer Critics Circle, and Clarence Derwent. Tonya's book *Get Over Yourself: How to Drop the Drama and Claim the Life You Deserve* was published by Hyperion in January 2006.

FIRED FACT

Odds that someone would continue in his current job if he won $10 million in the lottery: 1 in 3.[1]

REMEMBRANCE OF PORN PAST

Scott Carter

Now that I'm a civilian again, I sometimes think back to the time I worked in a place that my colleagues affectionately referred to as a pussy factory. How had this happened? I am, after all, a white Anglo-Saxon Puritan from Kansas City—the self-proclaimed Heart of America, where life imitated Art Linkletter. I lived on a street called State Line that separated the Kansas of Dorothy from the Missouri of Tom Sawyer. Ours was a no-problem culture, a Norman Rockwell hologram, a wildlife reserve for Republicans and Rotarians and Methodists for whom sex was a sublimation of the work impulse.

In 1976 I moved to New York to have greatness thrust upon me. By day I wrote comic plays and by night worked as a proofreader. I roomed with my younger brother Craig, a Columbia literature major who loved the bleak, brooding Puritan prose of Hawthorne and the grim life lessons of Shakespearean tragedy: how we get in earnest what we beg in jest, how we're hoist with our own petards, and how Shakespeare divided time into Holiday and Everyday and believed that while one could every once in a while indulge in Holiday, one must ultimately return to Everyday. Now, why was Craig like this? Astrologers might note his birthday (April 15), which of course is tax deadline, the sinking of the *Titanic*, and the death of Abraham Lincoln.

But I always traced his behavior back to our father and our father's father.

Our grandfather was a fun-fearing Iowa Presbyterian forever chastened by the Great Depression. He lived for Everyday, not Holiday. At Christmas he would remove anything that produced sounds or music from the presents our parents were planning to give us. He once left a New Year's Eve party at 11:45. When he died we found among his very neatly packed belongings three boxes: one marked Long String, one marked Short String, and a third marked Miscellaneous String.

My father, on the other hand, was a salesman who loved Holiday. He loved to pick up the check, tip big, and give surprise presents. By the time I was sixteen, my father was regularly coming into my room late at night to excitedly discuss religion and politics. I figured he was trying to relate to me, but later we were told that he was having a nervous breakdown.

To Craig, I think, Dad's fall confirmed Grandpa's caution; Everyday banished Holiday. And so I was dreamer to his drone and together we dwelt in a Manhattan apartment but really we were a thousand miles apart.

The New York I'd fantasized about was trading quips with S. J. Perelman while being feted by David Merrick at Sardi's. The New York I was getting was life with Bartleby the Scrivener. I reviewed the life scenarios of those I admired like a lawyer studying case precedents: I couldn't become a riverboat pilot like Mark Twain. Or join a whaling ship like Herman Melville. Maybe I should just disappear like Ambrose Bierce.

Instead I moved to L.A.

I'd never wanted to move to L.A.; I'd wanted to be a famous New York playwright lured reluctantly to L.A. like Ben Hecht. Hecht, who wrote *The Front Page* and *Twentieth Century* and had been wooed to Hollywood in 1926. His friend, writer-producer Herman Mankiewicz had telegrammed him promising "millions to be made [here] and your only competition is idiots." Now, I was willing to make millions. And compete with idiots. But I had no friends like Herman Mankiewicz. I had friends like Stoney—a film student from the University of Arizona who liked to get stoned and listen to Thin Lizzy and who revered impoverished Indian tribes for their vast insights and strong hallucinogens. Like everyone else in L.A., Stoney had his own independent production company, but the best my personal Mankiewicz could do for me was to show me an ad he'd read in the *Valley News* for "Adult and Humor Editors."

That's how I came to be interviewed by Jonathan—a hyperintense twenty-three-year-old chain-smoker who hired me to write soft-core pornography, I think because I was articulate and asthmatic like his hero, Marcel Proust.

Having failed to gain admission into the New York literary pantheon, dropped out of college, and flunked my draft physical, I saw the porn mill as a further descent down the hole I'd dug for myself. That first day of work I had anticipated being greeted by Hawthornian witches, a coven of depraved syphilitic monsters chanting, "You'll be hoist on your own petard. You'll get in earnest what you begged in jest."

Instead, on my first morning on the job, I pulled up to a one-story, red-brick building in an industrial park by a railroad track. There was no name above the glass-door entrance to our building. The offices were a string of linoleum-floored suites with cheap paneling and fluorescent lights. I walked into the art room. Rock music blasted from a radio, and the room was cluttered with artists' T squares, triangles, and X-Acto knives. The "artists" had their own dartboard, craps table, and a refrigerator stuffed with sweet, fattening junk food. But what really caught my eye were the pictures that covered the four walls: vagina! vagina! penis! vagina! breast! anus!—everywhere!—like glossy wallpaper.

I took one look at the adult playroom that first morning and thought, I've dug all the way through the earth and come out not just in China but in the Forbidden City! Craig was wrong! This paid Holiday would eclipse Everyday—forever! A Puritan's dream. I would be requested, nay, required, to explore that which my culture ignored and condemned. I could wallow in smut and none dare call me pervert. Viva la work ethic!

I worked on the soft-core side, which was physically separated from hard-core by a hallway and metaphorically by penetration.

The drill was simple: the photographers shot models and gave the pictures to the artists, who laid out the pages leaving space for the writers. We had four rules: we couldn't refer to rape, murder, bestiality or imply that models were underage. We published ninety different titles, some going back thirty years. According to Jonathan, soft-core readers remained loyal to what got them off at puberty. If that was a shapely gam in an elegant stocking, fine. They didn't want to see it all.

Hard-core readers did. The hard-core editor and my future girlfriend was Liz, a divorcée from the Bronx, who studied literature at Vassar and loved writing porn. My three favorite titles of hers were a Gershwin parody called *Picture Me Sucking You*, a hard-core book simply named *Another Fucking Magazine*, and *Second Coming*, the poignant tale of a bride who returned from the dead to fuck her widowed husband one last time— only a dream . . . or was it? The haunting final gauzy image was of an artificial rose dotted with one lonely teardrop of semen.

So that was work. But it never seemed like work. Oh, sometimes we'd have to pretend to be working when Eddie, the creative director, came into the editorial room. Eddie held monthly meetings to plot the fetish strategies for the upcoming magazines. Tits and ass; ass and tits. No matter what the theme, something was about to be inserted somewhere by somebody at the end of each story. It was as inevitable as a shootout at the end of a western. As Eddie himself once said to me, "Remember, Scotty, tits and ass is our meat and potatoes."

The junior soft-core writer was a Vietnam vet called Tex. "*Yee-haw!*" was his mantra. Tex thought "bust" meant breast and that every woman had two! Tex thought "discretion" was a bodily function! Tex thought New England was a state! Tex thought one was half of four! Tex sold speed tablets to Liz for thirty cents apiece that he'd bought three for a dollar—and thought he was making a profit! One time I asked him which wild animals are monogamous and he replied, "You mean big titted?"

Though Jonathan was boss and I had seniority over Tex, he was a better scum scribe than either of us. His writing was terse and crude. Mine was convoluted and absurd. In one of my books you'd see pictures of a model on her back with her ankles around her ears and the caption would read

> *Edna's favorite philosophers used to be the British empiricists—Locke, Berkeley, and Hume—but now she says: "Hell, it's all just a footnote to Plato . . ."*

To my colleagues, I think I was an enigma (a word Tex confused with *enema*). While my coworkers wore jeans and T-shirts, I dressed in rumpled suits and fedoras, for I was a slumming East Coast exile—in L.A. but not of L.A. As my respect for New York had intimidated me, so my contempt for L.A. freed me. I could reinvent myself in this mecca for amnesiacs. I had a girlfriend, a writing job, a sense of humor, and hope. Back in Arizona, my friends thought I had a very cool job, and my parents told our relatives in Kansas City that I was editing textbooks.

One morning Eddie called me into his office: "Scotty, you gotta make your writing harder. Not that it ain't good. It just may not be for us. Can't you take out the wit?"

So to override my ambivalence I wrote a poem and posted it above my typewriter.

> **We Stoop to Serve**
> *Omit the wit.*
> *Look at it. Love it.*
> *Write fast. Write hard. Write down.*
> *Do not rewrite.*
> *Do not write three lines*
> *Without writing:*
> *Pecker, prick, dick, dong, cock, balls,*
> *Clit, cunt, twat, snatch, pussy,*
> *Tit, nipple, knocker, boob,*
> *Ass, anus, hole, butt,*
> *Screw, suck, cum, fuck.*
> *They're gonna pay you Friday.*

My attempts at humor did not go over well. One day Eddie called me into his office to rebuke me for comparing a model's breasts to the cupolas of St. Basil's Cathedral in Red Square: "Humor is not what our reader breaks his hump to pay his hard-earned money for! Laughter distracts him from his erection, which is his main concern! Everything else is bullshit. We must respect the fact that our reader is demented!"

Not long after that, Eddie called me into his office.

"Scotty, I have some bad news."

I saw a pay envelope in his hand.

"The order was to cut back, it's just that simple . . . You'll get unemployment and a week of vacation. Scotty, you're too intelligent for smut. Don't waste your life in it."

I walked through the gallery of glossy wallpaper for the last time and cleaned out my desk. Tex helped—but with a little too much enthusiasm. I told myself I was fine and it turned out I was. By Monday morning I had answered ads, made my calls, and mailed out resumes. Only a few weeks later it would be incredible to me that every day I had walked through the gallery seeing not a vagina, a penis, or a breast (those are organs that belong to people) but simply a cunt, a cock, a tit. After my mere few weeks at the pussy factory, the pictures had completely lost their impact on me. I had become as blasé as a battlefield doctor examining a shrapnel wound. I realized that my brother Craig had been right all along. Holiday always reverts to Everyday.

Scott Carter is an Emmy-nominated producer/writer of HBO's *Real Time with Bill Maher* and, before that, *Politically Incorrect.* He lives in Los Angeles with his wife, Bebe, and their two daughters, Calla and Cary.

FIRED FACT

Number of employees terminated by "Neutron" Jack Welch: 118,000

Welch received the nickname "Neutron Jack" because (like the bomb of the same name) he eliminated people but kept buildings intact. Welch fired 118,000 people in his first few years as head of General Electric but was eventually named Manager of the Century by *Fortune* magazine.[2]

LAST SHIFT AT THE FETISH DELI

Mark Haskell Smith

"Hand me a female spoon."

I hadn't really worked in the restaurant that long, maybe four or five months, and I didn't know all the lingo, the jargon, the fryolator patois of the hardened restaurant professional. I definitely didn't know what a female spoon was. The manager, John, squinted his eyes and glared at me. He wasn't that much older than I was—he was twenty-four and I was seventeen—yet he carried his portly little body with all the grace and good humor of a pissed-off drill sergeant—Jack Webb meets the Pillsbury Doughboy.

"A fucking female spoon. While I'm young."

Optimistically I handed him a ladle. He scowled at me, then bowled forward and snagged a slotted spoon off the counter. He waved the spoon in my face.

"You did finish high school? Right? You're not a complete moron?"

I nodded. Kind of like a moron might nod.

My girlfriend at the time was an amateur hippie, a proto-feminist, and a soon-to-be lesbian. She would've been outraged hearing gender stereotypes applied to cooking utensils; she would've stood up and done something; she would've protested, launched a boycott against all delis with fun-sounding names, brass railings, and hanging ferns. She would have marched on Washington. But I couldn't quite summon the courage to inform John that he was being sexist.

"I thought it was called a slotted spoon."

He nodded, as if that proved his point. "You would."

I never intended to pursue a career in the exciting field of line cookery. As much as I enjoyed building a club sandwich—skewering it together with toothpicks dressed festively with little bursts of colored plastic—or smashing a fat Reuben down on the grill, this was just something I was doing over the summer before I went off to college. The grease that hovered in the air was bad for my skittish teenage skin. The fryers and slicers made me nervous.

Then there was John. If he had been your run-of-the-mill, garden-variety asshole, I could've handled him. But John had a sick and twisted game he liked to play with his employees: a heady mix of ritual humiliation and fetishism. He kept a strict "clean shave" policy. Beards, mustaches, even long sidebums were forbidden, and male employees were required to shave even the lightest stubble clean before coming to work. Even though my fuzz was more nectarine than peach, I adhered to the clean shave dogma. The last thing I wanted was to face "the blade."

His twisted little game went like this: John would approach an employee, a busboy or a waiter, a dishwasher or a line cook, and say, "You forgot to shave." At this point he would produce an ancient and decrepit disposable razor from his pocket, wave it in front of the guy's face, and tell him to go into the bathroom and shave. John had been managing the restaurant for two years and was proud to still be using the original razor. The employee/victim would hang his head, mutter something unintelligible, and go into the bathroom. He would return, face spotted with bits of slowly reddening toilet paper stuck on to staunch the hemorrhaging from the various nicks, cuts, and abrasions caused by the dull blade. John would take back the razor, hold it up in the air like it was Excalibur, and remind everyone to shave before coming to work. It was, he said, company policy and a "public health issue." Refusal to shave was grounds for dismissal. I can only imagine that he went home at night and masturbated while holding the razor and dreaming about freshly shaved skin.

My night of long knives came on the day of the female spoon.

John lifted his poached egg out of the water and looked over at me. "You forgot to shave."

I touched my face reflexively. "No. I shaved this morning."

John leaned in, taking a closer look. "Doesn't look like it."

"I did."

John whipped out the razor. "Do it again."

"But I did shave. Honest."

"Do it or you're out of here."

Like many stubbly men before me I shuffled into the bathroom and turned on the hot water and took a long look at myself in the mirror. I held the razor blade up in the light and studied the jagged, rusty, hair-, skin-, blood-encrusted thing and I realized something about myself, something that is true to this day: I have a problem with authority figures.

I walked out of the bathroom and handed him back the razor. "Can't do it."

"What?"

"I'm not going to do it."

John glared at me. The waiters, cooks, dishwashers, busboys, cashiers—they all turned to watch. "Then you're fired."

When I arrived at college that fall, I had grown something that looked like an approximation of a beard—you know, the kind of wispy curls that look like a population density map of Wyoming, the kind of beard that just makes your face look vaguely dirty. As I tugged on my scraggly chin hairs, my feminist girlfriend informed me that she was moving out to live with a firefighter named Barbara and that, yes, Barbara could kick my ass so I shouldn't "be a baby about it." She was also taking all the cookware—the pots, pans, spatulas, and spoons. Even the female spoon was leaving.

Mark Haskell Smith is a screenwriter and the author of two novels, *Delicious* and *Wet*.

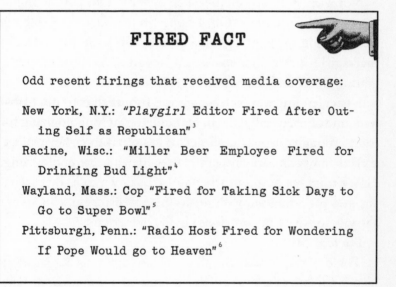

FIRED FACT

Odd recent firings that received media coverage:

New York, N.Y.: *"Playgirl* Editor Fired After Outing Self as Republican"[3]

Racine, Wisc.: "Miller Beer Employee Fired for Drinking Bud Light"[4]

Wayland, Mass.: Cop "Fired for Taking Sick Days to Go to Super Bowl"[5]

Pittsburgh, Penn.: "Radio Host Fired for Wondering If Pope Would go to Heaven"[6]

ATTRACTIVE IN A BAD WAY

Rob Cohen

Oh, shit.

Here she comes.

And it is with those five words that I have begun every single date in my life.

Not with "Oh, boy, here she comes" or "Oh, I am going to get sooo laid" or even "Oh, I hope I remembered to take my spastic colon medicine." None of that. It is with dread. Dread that a girl is exiting her apartment right now to come meet me, getting closer and closer to what I am already convinced will be a disaster, ending way too many hours sooner than it should and with one of us, usually me, in tears, desperately apologizing for what I thought was a compliment (kudos to the glass eye industry), then even more desperately apologizing for apologizing. Hey, I tried my best, but when it comes down to it, that's what she gets for going out with me in the first place. I mean, didn't she talk to any of my previous victi . . . girlfriends?

I'm *that* guy.

The one responsible for all those late-night crying jags. My face is on the labels of all those pints of Häagen-Dazs consumed during said jag, especially Rocky Road. I'm a date tornado, and when I touch down, I leave behind nothing but regret, distrust, and the odd cow in a tree. I'm the Date Grinch, but instead of stealing presents from Whos, I steal women's evenings, and their next five months' worth of interest in men.

So I am doing the only humane thing possible. I am firing myself from dating. I'm bad at it, I did horribly in it in school, and quite frankly, I've given myself plenty of warning, so this can't come as a complete surprise. If it's any consolation, I'm still young and have plenty of time to find a new occupation that better suits my abilities . . . or lack thereof, and on the plus side, I did make out with myself at the office Christmas party, so can almost certainly count on giving myself an excellent recommendation. There's only one small problem.

Tonight's date is coming out of her apartment lobby right now.

Damn it! Why do I keep putting myself in this position? Oh well. If I know me, I'll have plenty of time to answer that on our deathly quiet ride home from the restaurant/movies/arcade, the *click click* of my turn signal mercifully interrupting the silence of her rage.

But hold on a second. At this point you're probably thinking that I am fully to blame for this situation, that I have done this to myself. Not true, my friend. I am only half of the equation, for you see, when it comes to the ladies, I have the unfortunate delight of being . . . a freak magnet. "A what?" you say, putting down your nonfat, grande soy milk frappu-yummo for emphasis. "A freak magnet," I respond.

The guy who, for some unknown reason, assuming the government is not involved, seems to walk around emanating some sort of powerful beam from within that only attracts girls who are incredibly appealing on the outside, but sooooo not on the inside. Like a Godiva's chocolate . . . full of scorpions with diarrhea. You know the kind.

They're the girls who make a whole group of people laugh at a party but, when the group whittles down to just the two of you, instantly begin talking about how they came there straight from "night therapy" or how a close family member did something *highly* inappropriate to them at their confirmation/bat mitzvah/third birthday party or simply say, "Your aura smells like Christmas" and stare at you. For half an hour. And staring not with normal eyes but with eyes with a crazy spiral in the middle, like those old X-ray specs from the backs of comic books.

"Hey, what happened to that funny, charming girl from a few seconds ago?" I want to ask her. "Because this new chick is scaring the just-gobbled taquitos out of me." But I don't. I just smile, nod my head in agreement, and let the crazy times roll. And you want to know why?

Because that's exactly what makes this girl interesting to me. Isn't that sick?

Believe me, I know, but it's true. "Normal" girls offer nothing except security, open communication, and unconditional love, and who in their right mind wants that? Certainly not me, because that would be too healthy, aka *booooooo*ring!

I like a little excitement in my dating, something to keep me on my toes. You tell me who doesn't enjoy waking up in the middle of the night to find your girl tearfully beating the crap out of you with her oversized "dream journal," screaming, "Stop betraying my energy, Uncle Lou!"

I'm waiting.

A little backstory. Back to where this nightmare began. Where my dangerous addiction to shaky women and even shakier excuses started.

Fade in: a small western prairie town in Canada:

Jennifer Molero, September 9–17, 1979
We went on two dates at the beginning of tenth grade, and she told me before we went any further, she wanted to hear those three special words. I told her we'd only gone out twice, that it seemed a little soon, and jokingly said that I too would like to hear three special words, but they happened to be "Please wel-

come *Kiss*!" The only thing I remember after that was her face getting very red, the words "Die, sperm canister!" and a stiletto heel coming toward me a little too quickly.

Her whereabouts are unknown, but I have never felt the same about high heels . . . or *Kiss*.

Deanna Sharpe, June 14–August 9, 1981
I met her at my friend's sixteenth birthday party, where she spent all night kneading my ass faster than an epileptic pizza maker manipulating a ball of dough, then dragged me into a closet and jammed my hand up her shirt. I happily took her cue, but when I tried to kiss her, she ran out of the closet, screaming that I had attacked her. After everyone calmed down, it turned out she had been "attacked" by five other boys that night, by one twice.

We went roller-skating the next Saturday.

Karla Shapiro, May 1, 1985
Totally cool, great sense of humor, gorgeous body, and fantastic attitude toward life.

Not my cup of tea.

Nikki Sanderson, April 29–December 31, 1987
Had a great eight months together, until New Year's Eve rolled around and she told me she wanted to fulfill her secret fantasy of having sex . . . in the tub . . . and climaxing exactly at the stroke of twelve . . . while watching *Dick Clark's Rockin' New Year's Eve*.

Unfortunately between my tiny apartment tub, the somewhat prohibitive water, and the TV's being in the other room, we missed our target by a few seconds.

She became incredibly upset, but I told her if it made her feel any better, the Dick Clark show was actually taped weeks earlier. It didn't.

We got back together in time for next New Year's Eve, but her interest in aqua-sex and surprisingly, Dick Clark, had waned.

And the list, like my collection of filed restraining orders, goes on and on. Winter turned to spring, spring turned to summer, but the lure of the unwell was still my year-round passion.

But enough of the horrible past. I need to deal with the horrible present.

Tonight's date is now just a few feet away.

She's at the curb.

Time for the obligatory leap out of the car, an overeager hand ready to open her door, time to usher her into the Regret-mobile, with a smile that says, "I am so so sorry." Set your disappointment clock, Sally, because it's go time. The date has begun, my last date ever, where I am no doubt about to embark on yet another fruitless evening of witty banter, eclectic personal experiences, and then dashed hopes as she asks me back to her apartment, where I catch a glimpse of her massive, picnic-table-length mood swing medication collection and then myself in the hallway mirror, as I run out the door.

But you know what? Now that I think about it, maybe firing myself was a bit too hasty. Maybe I should give the kid another shot. Maybe somewhere out there, on this great big beautiful green ball we call Earth but the preinvasion alien scouts posing as various world leaders call Future Slave Colony 5, there is someone right for me. A woman who has a great sense of humor, but not at my car's expense. A woman who doesn't burst into tears when you ask her to the movies because "it's too dark in there." A woman who likes spontaneous fun, but not with anything marked "Warning: Do not use anally."

A woman whom I would want to go on a vacation with, a vacation that I could feel at least 75 percent confident will be relaxing, not an opportunity for me to meet the local police "jumper negotiator" every evening and be encouraged to tell my lady through a bullhorn that the honor bar in our room didn't tell her she can fly.

So I make this promise to myself. I'm back on the job, but with one change. No more nuts. Freak magnet be damned. From now on if a girl can even spell *wacky*, she's gone.

I need to look out for number one, to put an end to this madness of madness and find the one healthy, normal, funny lady out there who will bring me years of companionship and delight and provide that rare feeling of knowing that she is there for me 24/7 and that I can trust her with my most personal of thoughts.

And who knows. Tonight's date might just be her.

"So, what do you feel like doing this evening?" I ask.

She smiles, playfully flips back her gorgeous hair, and says, "I don't care, just so long as you remind me to take the pills that will stop me from biting off your penis."

Helloooooooo, Mrs. Cohen.

Rob Cohen has been a writer and producer of Emmy-winning *The Ben Stiller Show, The Simpsons,* and *Just Shoot Me,* among other jobs he has held. The pride of the Canadian Rockies, Robert Cohen loves honesty, cold Chinese food, long walks in the rain, and short, ambiguous bios.

CAPPI'S PIZZA AND SANGWEECH SHOP

Carl Capotorto

When I first started thinking about the many times I've been fired, several stories sprang to mind. But I've decided not to tell them. I mean, there was my first job out of college at a place called Photo Resources, which I got fired from for knocking my boss's wig off her head with a pointer. I don't know how it happened. One minute I was handing her the pointer (really a window pole) and the next minute her wig was hanging off the end of it. A few minutes later I was handed my pink slip. In all fairness, that hadn't been my first offense. I had also destroyed the company's copier and fax machine by making a pot of coffee but forgetting to put the pot in place. Fresh coffee, piping hot, streamed onto the fax machine and rolled down into the vents of the copier, destroying both machines faster than you could say, "Freshen your cup, anyone?" (It was their own fault really, for having the coffeemaker in the copy area.) But this story is mundane. And it's a downer. So I've decided not to tell it.

Then there was the time I got fired from a long-term temp assignment at Arthur Andersen (guess who got the last laugh on that one) for mixing up a mailing and sending some trade secrets to the wrong client. I walked into my cubicle one morning, bright-eyed and chipper, only to find the entire contents of my desk and walls being loaded into a giant Dumpster. An extra pair of shoes I had stashed in the bottom drawer, snowflake cutouts I had pinned cheerfully here and there, a few dozen copies of my plays along with several copies of, well, my butt—all of it being dutifully trashed by custodial services. I demanded that I be allowed to retrieve my belongings and was instead escorted out of the building under heavy security. (I still miss those china red Hush Puppies with the silver buckles.) This episode I find humiliating. Plus I can't be sure that my little clerical error didn't contribute to the company's ultimate demise. So I won't be sharing that one either.

Of course there was also the time I got fired from another long-term temp assignment, this one at Bankers Trust. I was working for a man named Don Uhline and had trouble answering his phone: "Don Uhline's line." I kept saying "Dine Uhlon's len" or "Den Uhlone's lane" or other such variations. The end came when a woman named Elaine LaLanne called and I had to buzz him and say, "Mr. Uhline, Elaine LaLanne on the line." It came out all twisted up. Don had had enough. I was fired before lunch. But I got the better of him. While he was on his way up to HR to have me bagged, I slipped into his office, spat on the rug, and put an old Sicilian curse on his head taught to me by my Calabrese grandma. She told me never to speak of the curse in public. So I won't.

The story on the theme of being fired that mostly fills my mind is how my father used to fire customers from the ill-fated pizza shop he owned for a few years in our native Bronx. Cappi's Pizza and Sangweech Shop (where the motto was "We Don't Spel Good, Just Cook Nice") was a very dark episode in the life of my family, hardly appropriate as essay fodder. It was a failure and nearly bankrupted us. But it might have worked out differently had my father been more welcoming to his customers.

First of all, when you walked in you were greeted by a ten-foot hand-painted sign that read This Is Not a Basketball Court, followed by a long list of noes written in fat red letters: No Running, No Pushing, No Shouting, No Yelling, No Fighting, No Cursing, No Grabbing, No Shoving, No Strollers, No Bicycles, No Roller Skates, No Special Orders, No Extra Cheese, No Slices at the Table.

This last rule caused no end of drama. The shop was divided into two sections. One half was a typical pizza counter, the other was a small dining room with little Formica tables and travel posters of Italy on the walls. Here you could order all kinds of obscure Italian delicacies, like *capozelle* (which is the baked, stuffed head of a goat), *sanguinuccio* (buckets of animal blood that they boil and sweeten and churn into a nauseating mock-chocolate pudding), and *zuppa di trippa* (the lining of a cow's stomach stewed in tomato sauce). My mother, my poor mother, was in charge of the kitchen.

These two areas, the pizza counter and the dining room, were completely separate domains in my father's mind. So if a family of three comes in for dinner, say, and Mom orders the eggplant parmigiana, Dad'll have the shrimp oreganata, and Little Junior just wants a slice of pizza, guess what? No Slices at the Table. Little Junior's going to have to be forcibly separated from his family, sent outside to enter the pizza area through a separate door, and made to stand at the counter to eat his slice alone. The only thing missing was a dunce cap. The parents, of course, would object. Then my father, ever the people pleaser, would throw them out. He'd argue with them for a minute or two and then pull a full-throttle Ralph Kramden: *"Out! Get ouuut!"* These poor people just wanted a little dinner. Word spread. The dining room remained empty.

To fill it, my father had the bright idea of offering to throw pizza birthday parties. So a poor, unknowing parent would book the place for a Saturday afternoon and load in ten or twenty screeching eight-year-olds. Long before the first pizza was served (full pies at the table were acceptable, by the way, just no slices), Cappi would be throwing the entire party into the street. Again with the Ralph Kramden: *"Out! All of you! Get ouuut!"* My own tenth birthday party ended this way when

Johnny Appelbaum starting popping balloons with a plastic fork. *"That's it! Party's over! Out! Ouuuut!"*

In 1965, our local movie theater, the Globe, became a porno house. Its first offering was *I Am Curious (Yellow)*. This enraged my father and he began a campaign to shut the theater down. It soon grew into a broader crusade against all pornography and before long he founded the Committee to Control Obscenity by Constitutional Means. I still have the letterhead. The address? Number 2259 White Plains Road, Bronx, New York. Cappi's. Yes, Cappi's Pizza and Sangweech Shop was the national headquarters of the Committee to Control Obscenity by Constitutional Means.

When he wasn't flying up to Albany in his heavily backfiring lime green Cadillac to lobby members of the state legislature to add antipornography provisions to the U.S. Constitution, Cappi was proselytizing from behind the pizza counter. "How do you feel about pornography?" he'd ask every adult male customer. Most of them felt it was a matter of free speech. "Oh yeah? Is *this* free speech?" And he'd flash a picture of, like, a nun standing in a barnyard with her habit hiked over her head, being violated by a farm animal. (He kept a store of particularly egregious porn samples handy for just this purpose.) "Or *this*?" And it would be a super close-up of some way-dilated bodily orifice being violated by an oversized household object, like a vacuum cleaner hose or a decorative vase. Of course the people would be horrified. They'd politely explain that while these images weren't their cup of tea, they didn't have to see them if they didn't want to (unless, of course, they were trying to order a slice of pizza at Cappi's) and that therefore the images had a right to exist. This kind of bleeding heart liberal attitude really raised my father's ire and he'd toss them out. "Well, you know what? I don't serve perverts here. Now *get ouuuut*!" Another potential customer fired from Cappi's. I'd say one out of three potential customers of Cappi's was tossed out into the street before even placing an order. Needless to say, we were out of business in just a few years.

The site of Cappi's Pizza and Sangweech Shop is now a combination taco joint and karate studio. My former bosses at Arthur Andersen are behind bars. I like to think that Don Uhline of Bankers Trust is begging for change on a back street somewhere, doomed forever for reasons he will never understand. Photo Resources has long been rendered obsolete by the digital age. And so I find that there's not one story on the theme of being fired that I can tell without causing trouble for myself or others. So I respectfully decline to write on this topic. But thank you for asking.

Carl Capotorto is a writer and actor who lives in New York. He plays Little Paulie Walnuts on *The Sopranos* on HBO.

FIRED FACT

Producer Gavin Polone (*Curb Your Enthusiasm*) on being fired from a talent agency: "They padlocked my office, my assistant was crying, and they were literally trying to take the Rolodex out of my hands as I was escorted from the building. The best thing was that they forgot to turn off my company phone and back then, this was in 1989, your car phone bill could run eight hundred dollars a month. I wound up using it for four months."[7]

Subject: No More Rain Days
From: Janet M. Lorenz
Date: March 16, 2005, 2:44 P.M., CST
To: daytoday@npr.org

I got fired from my first job as a lifeguard at the Stony Creek Pool in Reading, Pennsylvania. It was one of the most positive and influential experiences of my teenage years. I was sixteen, five feet six inches tall, muscularly lean, and tan, and I had long golden hair and green eyes. I was rather a serious, hardworking girl who loathed the label "airhead." The firer, male, nineteen, was the pool manager. My sharp-as-a-tack memory—should you think I am fuzzy on the details from 1974—recalls his height as average, build as nonmemorable, hair as curly strawberry blond, eyes brown, and skin pimply and tan resistant. His behavior? Lecherous.

One morning in early July as I was netting leaves off the pool's surface, he got too close to my Speedo-clad posterior and crooned over my shoulder, "When you're done with that you can come and clean my office." My stomach muscles contracted, causing the cinnamon toast within to toss some dust into my throat. "Asshole," I sputtered.

"*What* did you say?" He moved several paces farther from me on the concrete catwalk, turned around, and said, "I dare you to walk right up to my face and say that again."

I dropped the net into the pool and glanced over to the parking lot to check the distance between my '72 Chevrolet Nova and the pool's entrance. The car was close. I walked up to him and we faced each other in a bitter stare. I glanced over at my car again and stepped in closer. Standing six inches from ripe whiteheads and a sunburned forehead, I took a deep diver's breath and exhaled "asshole." I think it wasn't the uttering of "asshole" that actually got me fired. After all, I was just taking him up on a dare. I think it was the end of my exhale that hit him like a cold shower on his jumpy boy parts. Call it feminine wiles or offended teen girl posturing, but nobody can end an exhale with one of those "you bore me" sighs like a woman can. I had never deployed this skill so assertively before this moment, but I came to practice and perfect it over the years in my management consulting career.

So, staring back at me, he fired me. I felt great. My first real feminist experience and I thought it had gone, well, swimmingly. He looked insecure and like a peanut in his black nylon swimmer's brief. I felt like Sekhmet, the Egyptian sun goddess, sometimes called the Mistress of Dread. Not only had I stood my ground, I actually had a job lined up at the YMCA with my best girl pal, Cathy. "Forty hours a week, paid. No rain days!" she said of the indoor job. And we would be in charge of the pool area. More money, more responsibility. I liked this whole idea of being fired for standing on principle. And I could work on my late summer tan on the weekends.

As I departed Stony Creek Pool, I poked my head into the manager's office and said, "I'll have to tell my dad why I no longer work here. When he learns the real reason why you fired me, he might want to talk with you." Call that security backup. If the police use it, why shouldn't I?

And I left him to listen to the fading sounds of my rubber flip-flops snapping against my bare heels.

Janet M. Lorenz is a yoga teacher in Philadelphia, Pennsylvania.

RECIPE FOR THE RECENTLY REDUNDANT

Walter Scheib

When you leave a job, regardless of the circumstances, it's a time of some introspection. You take inventory of what you do well, the success you have had, and in my case the people who were there for me before I had any notoriety. One of the people I thought back to was Barbara Tropp from the China Moon Café in San Francisco. She challenged me to rethink many of my assumptions about cooking and life and made me a better person for having known her. So at this milepost in my career, thinking back to the values and abilities she let me know I had, I feel much better about my ability to climb the next mountain.

When my White House tenure ended, this is the dish I made. It is happy and light in taste and appearance, qualities you want to radiate when going out to get the next job. It has a little snap of spice to liven you up as you prepare for your next adventure. With this meal my wife and I toasted our old friend, reflected on past success, and anticipated future challenges. We drank Roederer White House Cuvée sparkling wine, of course, and we thought of good times to come.

Chef Scheib is busy with speaking engagements and is writing a book based on his culinary experience in the Clinton White House. Unlike members of the White House staff who maintain the fiction that resigning was their decision, Executive Chef Walter Scheib 3rd minced no words saying he had been fired. "It has been an honor to serve the first family," he added.[8]

Seared Scallops with Red Curry Sauce in the Manner of an Old Friend

Serves eight

Scallops

1 tablespoon minced ginger

1½ teaspoons chopped Chinese black beans

1½ teaspoons minced garlic

½ teaspoon chili paste

1 tablespoon Thai basil, finely cut

1 tablespoon sesame oil

1 tablespoon soy sauce

1 teaspoon fresh lime juice

2 to 3 large diver scallops per person

1. In a stainless-steel bowl combine all ingredients except scallops and mix well.

2. Add scallops and let marinate for 1 to 2 hours.

Vegetables

1 head baby bok choy per person

3 ounces each peeled carrots and peeled daikon

3 ounces each zucchini and yellow squash skin

1. Clean and split the bok choy.

2. Use a mandoline to slice the carrots and daikon and zucchini and yellow squash skin into long ribbons. Set aside.

Dressing

¼ cup peanut oil

2 tablespoons fresh lime juice

1 tablespoon minced ginger

1 tablespoon minced garlic

1 teaspoon chili paste

1. In a bowl combine dressing ingredients. Set aside.

Curry Sauce

1 tablespoon corn oil

4 to 5 roma tomatoes, quartered

5 oil-packed sun-dried tomatoes

1 tablespoon lemongrass, grated

½ tablespoon Thai chili, minced

1 tablespoon rice vinegar

1 tablespoon minced garlic

1 to 2 tablespoons red curry paste

Chicken stock

1 to 2 ounces unsweetened coconut milk

1. Heat the corn oil in a sauté pan. Add the roma tomatoes and cook over high heat until slightly charred.

2. Drain charred tomatoes. Put tomatoes, sun-dried tomatoes, lemongrass, chili, rice vinegar, garlic, and curry paste in a food processor and blend until smooth.

3. Transfer mixture to a stockpot. Add enough chicken stock to bring mixture to a saucelike consistency.

Garnish

Scallions, cut in julienne

Cilantro, cut in julienne

Rice vinegar

Salt

Pepper

Assemble Dish

1. In a medium-size nonstick pan, sear the marinated scallops until just cooked through, about 1½ minutes per side. Keep scallops warm.

2. Steam the bok choy until tender.

3. Stir-fry carrots, daikon, and zucchini and squash skin until cooked al dente.

4. Place cooked bok choy and other vegetables into a bowl and coat lightly with dressing.

5. Heat sauce. Add coconut milk to taste.

6. Place vegetables in center of a warmed serving plate.

7. Arrange scallops on top of vegetables.

8. Ladle sauce around edge of plate. Drizzle sauce over scallops.

9. Garnish with scallions and cilantro.

10. Season to taste with rice vinegar and salt and pepper.

THE FIRED SONG

Roy Zimmerman

Roy Zimmerman is a satirical singer-songwriter. The *Los Angeles Times* has referred to him as a "latter-day Tom Lehrer."

THE LETTER YOU WISH YOU'D SENT TO YOUR BOSS! NOW YOU CAN!

(Circle the sentiments that apply, cut on the dotted line, mail. You may want to leave your return address off the envelope!)

Dear *Mentor / Boss man / Tyrant:*

Working for you was a constant source of *inspiration / acid reflux / misery.*

I guess my mind was on *my true career goals / Christian decency / strangling you,* and that is why ultimately this was *a difficult / an impossible / a soul-stealing* job for me. I am so sorry I couldn't *fulfill your expectations / work for your miserly salary / cover your pathetic ass.* I hope to be able to *thank you / forgive you / screw you over* one day as my way acknowledging the *opportunity / heartbreak / career suicide* you afforded me.

I credit you for creating such a *stimulating / antediluvian / paranoid* work environment. I know you were consciously trying to be *supportive / intimidating / backstabbing* to all those *in your employ / under your thumb.* I will miss your *erudite sense of humor / inappropriate sexual advances / passive-aggressive personal style / bad puns / drunken rants* and *compassionate leadership / complete ineptitude / reign of terror.* Please forgive me for *resigning my position / egging your Mercedes / sending you dog poo.* I just couldn't leave without expressing my *regrets / anger / rage.*

I was truly *sad / relieved / joyous* when I got your *phone call / memo / Post-it* informing me I was *let go / fired / out on my ass.*

Wishing you *well / much needed luck / a slow and merciless death,*

Your *friend / foe / avowed enemy,*

NOTES

Who Came Up with the Phrase "You're fired"?

1. www.word-detective.com

1. The Job So Terrible You Can Only Hope to Be Fired

1. *Chicago Tribune*, March 23, 1998; Paul Grobman, *Vital Statistics* (New York: Plume, 2005).

2. http://www.courttv.com/people/2005/0812/koko_ctv.html.

3. Richard Kendall, *Van Gogh's van Goghs: Masterpieces from the van Gogh Museum, Amsterdam* (Washington, D.C.: National Gallery of Art, 1998).

4. *Christian Science Monitor*, March 9, 1999; *Financial Management*, December 2000; Grobman, *Vital Statistics*.

5. Robert Reich has a plan: He outlined his plan in a op-ed piece in the *New York Times* on September 3, 2005:

> The answer is a new compact that gives Americans enough security to accept economic change. Suppose, for example, lower- and moderate-income workers got a larger share of today's productivity gains through a much bigger Earned Income Tax Credit starting at, say, $6,000 for those who earned the least and gradually tapering off well into the middle class. This would go a long way toward easing the pocketbook concerns of Americans who are working harder but getting nowhere.
>
> To cushion the pain of job loss, unemployment insurance should be turned into reemployment insurance, helping people to get new jobs instead of keeping them waiting for old ones to return. Community colleges would do the retraining, in league with area businesses that identified skill shortages. Wage insurance would cover part of the difference between their old salary and their new starting wage.
>
> The new compact would also decouple health and pension benefits from unemployment, further reducing the negative impact of job loss. Employer-provided health insurance would be replaced with no-frills universal health under an expanded Medicare program, which could use its huge bargaining

leverage to extract lower costs from providers and drug companies. Lower-income workers would be encouraged to save for their retirement (over and above Social Security) by receiving several dollars from the government for every dollar they put away.

The price tag for the new compact won't be cheap. My back-of-the-envelope calculation is several hundred billion dollars a year. But given the high cost of our current doomed effort to turn back the global economic tides, it would more than pay for itself. By reducing the job insecurity felt by so many, a new compact would allow Americans to focus on embracing change instead of worrying about forever falling behind.

Robert Reich told me he doesn't really do his calculations on the back of an envelope. Well, once, but it was a little program, just a few million dollars. (I interviewed Professor Reich at Brandeis on September 6, 2005.)

6. *New York Post*, September 9, 2005.

2. The Firing You Didn't See Coming

1. Richard Layard, *Happiness: Lessons from a New Science* (New York: Penguin Press, 2005).

2. www.variety.com/article/VR1117928796, September 8, 2005.

3. You can get checks for up to 26 weeks. In many cases the compensation will be half your earnings, up to a maximum amount. Maximums vary from state to state. For example, in New York State you're entitled to collect up to a maximum of $405, which is half the state's average weekly wage, while in Arizona, the highest benefit rate is $205. In Washington State, the max is $496 a week. Your check is also affected by taxes: The Internal Revenue Service counts unemployment insurance benefits as income, so your check is taxable. Depending on the state, state and federal income tax can be withheld from your check. about.com, rates as of May 2005

4. http://en.wikipedia.org/wiki/Hieronymus_Colloredo.

5. "Another Marie Antoinette Moment," *New York Times*, January 2, 2006.

6. Bryan Harris, *The Sanctity of Marriage* (New York: Jeremy P. Tarcher, 2005). Interestingly enough, the "stallion ganglia" guy was radio personality Bill Ballance, who gave the conservative moralist Dr. Laura Schlessinger her big radio break as a regular commentator on his show. Bill and Laura (who was married at the time) also had a sexual relationship memorialized in photos he took and twenty-three years later posted on the Internet. Not long after this proof of her hypocrisy surfaced, her TV show was axed.

7. *The Wall Street Journal*, November 25, 2005; *New York Times*, November 17, 2005; www.boston.com/business/articles/2005/12/07/ford_to_lay_off_up_to_30000_workers; www.money.cnn.com/2005/11/21/news/fortune500/gm_cuts; www.xbox365.com/news.cgi?id=EpZVuuZyAFxbbnmPnl7693; www.rochesterdandc.com/apps/pbcs.dll/article?AID-/20050720/BUSINESS/50720001.

8. Ed Liebowitz, *New York Times*, August 28, 2005. Other fired directors include legendary director Howard Hawks, who said he quit as the director of *The Outlaw* in 1943, but the cinematographer said Hawks was fired by the producer. In 1960, on *Spartacus*, director Anthony Mann was fired and the studio hired the then-thirty-year-old director Stanley Kubrick, who himself had just been fired by Marlon Brando from the western *One-Eyed Jacks*. In 1976 John Avilden received an Oscar nomination for directing *Rocky* at about the same time he was fired as the director of *Saturday Night Fever*. In 1998 *Sid and Nancy* director Alex Cox was fired over clashes with writer Hunter S. Thompson from *Fear and Loathing in Las Vegas*. You can see this feud in the documentary *Breakfast with Hunter*, released in 2003.

9. *New York Times*, September 3, 2005, p. 114.

10. *New York Post*, September 9, 2005.

11. "Postcards from a Tax Holiday," *New York Times*, November 12, 2005.

3. The Time You Deserved to Be Fired

1. *Celebrity*, 1998.

2. *Manhattan*, 1979.

3. *Small Time Crooks*, 2000.

4. I really did believe that letter would arrive, embarrassingly. I checked my mail religiously for a month. It really got me thinking about how other people fire actresses, so I called one of the most successful producers in television, Steve Levitan, creator of *Just Shoot Me*, to see if he could, in essence, fire me better.

> **Annabelle:** Okay, Steve, I'm an actress and I'm guest-starring on your show and I'm getting every laugh, but you feel the whole story will work better if you had someone fatter/thinner/older/younger/more something less me, so you need to replace me. How do you fire me?
> **Steve:** I don't want anyone to feel bad, so you get the Lisa Kudrow story. Lisa was fired from the pilot of *Frasier*. Obviously she's extremely talented, but it was just the wrong role for her. Less than a year later she landed Phoebe on *Friends*, a role that ultimately made her rich and made

her a star. A role for which she would have been unavailable had she not been fired from *Frasier*.

Annabelle: Okay, I'm guest-starring on your show and I suck. I've blown every joke and handed you six pages of suggestions on how to make the show funnier. How do you fire me?

Steve: You get a call from your agent saying they're going a different way (and by "a different way," we mean with someone who doesn't suck or at least does so quietly).

Annabelle: Okay, I'm an actress and I'm completely drunk on the set. I've got my tongue down the craft service guy's throat and I keep blurting out, Who the fuck wrote this crap? How do you fire me?

Steve: Hmmm, drunk and horny. Whether I fired you would definitely depend on how hot you are.

Annabelle: Thanks, Steve. Gee I hope I get to be fired by you one day.

5. These statistics were arrived at by collating data from the U.S. Department of Labor at the bureau job opening and labor turnover survey information line, www.bls.gov/jlt/ and www.bls.gov/news.release/jolts.nr0.htm; for additional information call 202-691-5870.

6. Paul Grobman, *Vital Statistics* (New York: Plume, 2005).

7. Ibid.

8. http://money.cnn.com/2005/09/19/news/newsmakers/kozlowski_sentence/index .htm.

9. You can see why Ari Fleischer would be concerned with comments made by Bill Maher: A poll released earlier this year by the Pew Research Center for the People and the Press found that 21 percent of people aged eighteen to twenty-nine cited late night comedy shows as places where they regularly learned presidential campaign news. Even more startling is the change from just four years ago. When the same question was asked in 2000, Pew found only 9 percent of young people pointing to the comedy shows and 39 percent to the network news shows.

What Bill Maher actually said on *Politically Incorrect*: "We have been the cowards, lobbing cruise missiles from two thousand miles away. That's cowardly. Staying in the airplane when it hits the building, say what you want about it, it's not cowardly."

10. www.angelfire.com.

11. http://www.cnn.com/2005/WEATHER/09/01/katrina.fema.brown/index.html.

4. The Time Getting Fired Leads You to Something Better

1. I think the firee often remembers how he or she was fired more than the firer. Sybil Adelman Sage, who wrote on everything from *The Dick Van Dyke Show* to *Northern Exposure*, had this experience:

> I once thought there were three reasons you'd get fired—being incompetent, embezzling, or having sex with the wrong person in the office. I was wrong. None of my close encounters with being fired was for those reasons. They were all very different and have nothing in common except that I seem to be the only one who remembers what happened.
>
> I recall the day in 1971. I had been working as a secretary for Carl Reiner for five years when he called me into his office. Over the past few months I'd started writing episodes for television. "When I know you're at your desk working on your scripts," he said, "it's hard for me to interrupt you and ask you to do something."
>
> "I'm writing because I've got free time," I told him. I adored Carl, didn't believe I really had a writing career, and was terrified he'd say I should leave. "You're paying me. I'm here to do your work."
>
> Carl gave it another shot. "How can I ask you to sharpen pencils when you're in the middle of something?"
>
> "I'm happy to sharpen pencils," I countered, quipping, "or maybe you can use a pen." Carl didn't pursue it and let me stay until I was secure enough to leave. Thirty years later I can recall every word vividly but not Carl. When I recently reminded him of this he said, "Why would I want to get rid of you? You were a terrific secretary."
>
> You see, details of being fired, or even near-fired, are apparently embedded in the mind of the "firee" but no one else.
>
> And I'm sure the executive producer of the TV series I was later fired from would be equally unable to recall what he'd said after we'd been fired. My husband, Martin, and I had been writing partners for years by this point but we were reluctant to sign on for the long hours of staff work when we were offered a job on *Growing Pains*. Martin said yes, sure it would be canceled before you could say "Bialystock and Bloom."
>
> What we didn't count on was the teenybopper appeal of the young star of the show. Once the show went on the air, fan mail to Kirk Cameron overtook the reception area. And *Growing Pains* became our *Producers*. We

wanted out, preferring freelance work at home in grubby sweatpants so we could take breaks to make Play-Doh figures with our tiny son. While getting coffee one day, I came across one of the show's producers and surprised both of us by blurting out, "Is there a way we can get fired and still collect our money?"

He smiled. "That's the only thing they left for me to do." We worked out the specifics and hugged. "I'll go tell the executive producer I fired you," he said.

We were removing pictures from the bulletin board when Neal rushed in. "I heard what happened," he said, adding, "I wanted to be the one to fire you!"

Twenty years later I still can't come up with what would have been an appropriate response. I'm not sure why he said it, though I'm sure he has no memory of it!

(Sybil Adelman Sage and Martin Sage's son is now twenty-two. They no longer make Play-Doh figures, but they continue to receive writing assignments from people who once fired them.)

2. Gordon T. Anderson, "Want a big payday? Get fired," http://money.cnn.com/2003/04/29/pf/investing/ceo_severance/index.htm.

3. www.compensationresources.com/press-room/extreme-payoff--what-ceos-get-when-they.php

4. http://www.controller.ca.gov/search/search.asp?target=purcell&Search=Search&searchType=all

5. www.ecommercetimes.com/story/40594.html, accessed February 14, 2005.*

6. *Entertainment Weekly*, August 19, 2005.

7. *US Weekly*, May 25, 2004.

8. *USA Today*, December 26, 1989; Paul Grobman, *Vital Statistics* (New York: Plume, 2005). Martin was also fired by four other teams during his managing career.

9. Paul Laufer, ed., *The Health Anthology of American Literature*, 4th edition, vol. 2 (Boston: Houghton Mifflin, 2001).

10. *US Weekly*, May 25, 2005.

* The amounts of severance packages in notes 2 through 5 are the most up-to-date estimates at the time of printing. The actual amount may vary higher or lower depending on the stock values of each corporation and legal changes to the payouts.

11. Global Severances Package Survey, Right Management Consultants, according to their Web site "The world's leading career transition and organization consulting firm" (http://www.right.com).

12. *US Weekly*, May 25, 2004.

13. *New York Times*, November 10, 2002; Paul Grobman, *Vital Statistics* (New York: Plume, 2005).

14. *US News & World Report*, November 25, 2002; Grobman, *Vital Statistics*.

5. The Time You Had to Fire Yourself

1. Gallup Poll, August 29, 1997.

2. Jack Welch's management style included what he termed the 20,70,10 principle. He operated on the theory that in every company 20 percent should be rewarded, 70 percent motivated to improve their game, and 10 percent must be fired—no matter what their productivity. *The Baltimore Sun*, February 8, 2004; Paul Grobman, *Vital Statistics* (New York: Plume, 2005); www.usatoday.com/money/companies/management/2005=04=17=welch-advice_x.htm.

3. http://www.drudgereportarchives.com/data/2005/03/21/20050321/_151400_flash3pg1.htm.

4. http://www.wral.com/news/4191531/detail.html.

5. http://www.thebostonchannel.com/news/4437361/detail.html.

6. http://pittsburghlive.com/x/tribune-review/trib/pittsburgh/_323955.html.

7. *New York Times*, September 5, 2005.

8. *New York Times*, February 4, 2005. Statements from other White House departees included: Agriculture Secretary Ann Veneman ("time to move on to new opportunities"), Energy Secretary Spencer Abraham ("These four years have posed significant challenges on our family . . . and it will not be possible to continue to serve"), and Education Secretary Rod Paige ("time for me to return to Texas to attend to a personal project"). Treasury Secretary Paul O'Neill said, "He didn't care if people liked his work, he could be sailing around on a yacht." *The Washington Post*, December 6, 2002.

ACKNOWLEDGMENTS

This book had many supporters and people to thank, among them all the numerous wonderful writers whose stories are not included in this volume, including Eric Simonson, Rue McClanahan, David Rakoff, Charlene Woodard, Anthony Rapp, John Pankow, Theresa Rebeck, Matt Price, Patton Oswalt, Taylor Negron, B. D. Wong, Maggie Rowe, Mink Stole, John Fleck, Reno, Randy and Jason Sklar, Jenny Bicks, Jim Turner, Ron Orbach, Richard Vetere, Jimmy Pardo, Michaela Murphy, John Lehr, Orlando Jones, Craig Bierko, Emily Bergl, Anthony Haden-Guest, Steve Young, and Stephen Adly Guirgis.

"Crimes and Mythdemeanors" was first published in *Show People* magazine, winter 2004, with Erik Jackson editing, and was first performed at the Comedy Central Workspace at Jill Soloway and Maggie Rowe's Sit 'n Spin evening. Fired Tales of Jobs Gone Bad was developed at Comedy Central Workspace with the support of executives Gary Mann and Lauren Correo. The Second Stage Theatre productions were thanks to artistic director Carole Rothman, Tom D'ambrosio, and the tireless and inspired dedication of associate artistic director Chris Burney. L.A. Theatreworks productions continue thanks to artistic director Susan Loewenberg and associate artistic director Susan Raab Simonson. The *Fired* documentary film was produced by Richard Foos and Shout! Factory. (For information about upcoming shows and the *Fired* film, you can go to fired byannabellegurwitch.com.) Thank you John Moffitt, John Martin, Neil Pepe, John Ferraro, Larry Aidem, Candy Trabucco, Alice Spivak, Neena Beber and her guys Marc, Lucien, and Dashiell, Sara Sackner, Heather Winters, Lisa Gurwitch, Robert Morton, Dave Becky, Bernie Telsey Casting, Ryan

Maples, Marg Tabankin, Cyndi Stivers, Jason Zinoman, Reggie Cole at the AFL-CIO, Sara Sarasohn at *All Things Considered*, Steve Proffitt at *Day to Day* on NPR, Kent Black at the *Los Angeles Times Magazine*, Richard Foos and Shout! Factory, Randy Paul, Angus MacIndoe Restaurant, Laura Franklin and Kiehl's, Sybil and Martin Sage, Hillary Carlip and Fresh Yarn.com, Susan Kaufman, Lucinda Jenney, Patricia Heaton, Debbie Liebling, Chris Black, Talentworks, Paul Haas at the Endeavor Agency, and the levelheaded guidance of Kris Dahl at ICM. Alison Flierl, who helped proofread and was once fired by someone in a hospital bed who had just given birth only moments before! Thanks to Trish Todd, whose great fired story convinced me we should work together.

Special thanks to Woody Allen. I knew that working with you would change my life. It did. Just not in the way I expected.